MIND
BOSS

USING THE TENETS
OF **TOUGH THINKING**
TO TAKE CHARGE
OF YOUR THOUGHTS
& TRANSFORM YOUR LIFE

**EXECUTIVE BODYGUARD,
PERFORMANCE COACH
& WORLD RECORD HOLDER**
# MIKE GILLETTE

DENVER, COLORADO

Outskirts Press, Inc.
http://www.outskirtspress.com

ISBN: 978-1-4787-5337-7

Outskirts Press and the "OP" logo are trademarks belonging to Outskirts Press, Inc.

ACKNOWLEDGEMENTS

To my Lord and Savior Jesus Christ.

To my wife Tammie, whose belief in me made me believe.

To my Mother, gone too soon.

To my Father, who showed me that you can do anything provided you're willing to do the work.

To my second Mother, who taught me about unconditional love.

To those who have taught or encouraged me:
Chaplain (COL) Glenn Bloomstrom, Chris Smaby, George (Gil) Hansen, W. Hock Hochheim, Paul Vunak, Jerry & Fran Poteet, Guy Savelli, Leland Belding, Dennis Rogers, Chris Rider, Dan Kane, Lee Van Arsdale, James Sudderth, Jon Bruney, Tom & Donna Moretti.

TABLE OF CONTENTS

INTRODUCTION

Welcome to Mind Boss: Using the Tenets of Tough Thinking to Take Charge of Your Thoughts and Transform Your Life.

Sounds pretty good, doesn't it? A book that can actually teach you how to change the way you *think*?

Perhaps it even sounds a little *too* good.

Great. I want you to approach this book with a measure of skepticism. Within the "self-improvement" industry, there is just a lot of "fluff" (to put it politely).

So if you've been disappointed in the past by fancy-talking gurus, or you've tried to follow the convoluted advice of some would-be expert who has never actually "been there" or "done that," then **Mind Boss** may just be the book you've been waiting for.

The operative concept behind **Mind Boss** is a commitment to the intentional control of the mind. In this case, *your* mind. It is a simple enough idea to talk about, but to be able to actually make it happen seems far more elusive.

Many people are attached to the notion that we all live lives subject to the whims of random chance. And while it's true that much of what happens in life is beyond our control, we can always (if we *choose* to) control our own response to life's circumstances.

Think about all the people you know. Among them are people who just "get by." I'm not talking about just getting by financially, I mean that they are merely getting by in terms of the satisfaction they experience in their lives. They're not out pursuing their dreams. They may not even remember what their dreams were.

Now think about past conversations you may have had with those people. How many times did they complain about being overlooked at work? Or perhaps they complained of being singled out for unfair treatment?

How often have they had to apologize for reacting to situations inappropriately? Do they blow up? Have tantrums? Do they drink to excess and rationalize it later with statements like "You just don't know what I'm going through right now…"?

The behavior patterns I've just described are those of people who are not mentally tough. And people who aren't tough are seldom able to exercise control over their own lives. If you were to talk to them about the very idea of controlling either their temper or vocabulary, they might even offer further excuses, saying "Look, everyone gets mad. Everyone needs to let off some steam…."

This, of course, is true. We all get mad. We all need to release stress. But to conduct yourself in the manner I've been describing is to embody a *lack* of mental toughness.

And so many people live this way, captive not only to external circumstances, but also to the negative circumstances of their *own creation*. The idea of a self-determined future where you pursue goals with ruthless efficiency, is, for them, an alien concept.

So the sad result is that they go on, just getting by—all because they perpetually keep living **down** to their own expectations.

Well, if you want to do **more** than just get by, whether financially, creatively, socially, or otherwise, you need to live life with **assuredness,** with an **expectation of success**. And that's what **Mind Boss** is about: learning specific skills to help you *think* tougher.

The purpose of this book is to teach you how to take control of your mind and turn it into your most powerful "tool" for achievement. A tool that you can use to become tough, tough enough to pursue virtually anything you desire.

I will teach you my Tenets of Tough-Thinking for achieving what you want…for manifesting mental toughness in multiple areas of your life…for improving yourself each and every day.

Still skeptical? I understand. We live in a hype-intensive culture. Big promises are commonplace. And making good on those promises is far less common.

After all – most people constantly rationalize the positions they find themselves in (positions they do not necessarily like) and never really take control of their destiny.

But this process for achieving mental toughness is *proven*. I know it works, because it worked for me.

Allow me to explain…

I came from a broken home. I was a small, weak kid. We were poor. Both my mother and stepfather were captive to anger and alcohol and I was frequently left to fend for myself. My stepfather also beat my mother on a regular basis. Badly.

The outcome of my upbringing was that I became something of a loner, and I was fearful. I was especially afraid of violence.

By my mid-teens I looked to be a million miles away from being the kind of kid who would one day end up being strong and successful

Yet today – at 50+ years of age – I am just that. A success. A success because I have accomplished almost everything that I set out to do. This is what mentally tough people do. They pursue what is important. Important to them.

Success is something that *you* define. In my case, I turned my life around, developed a clear picture of my future, and hunted that future with relentless persistence.

After serving in the military and graduating from college, I entered the field of law enforcement. I was hired at a smallish agency in the middle of no place special. At that time, there was nothing to suggest that I would do anything other than work as a police officer until the age of 55 and then retire. And *at that time*, I would have been happy doing just that.

I had set some fitness records during the police academy and was honored as the distinguished graduate of my class. After completing my probationary period I was selected to attend a fitness instructor training course. It was unusual for a brand-new officer to be selected to be a trainer of other department personnel, but between my academy performance and my growing reputation as "that rookie who is always working out," I was picked to go.

Attending that training course made it abundantly clear to me that I loved teaching. And it seemed that I had most of the attributes to be good at it. In those days I also reasoned that if you were an instructor of something, you were circumstantially compelled to be better at it than everyone else. And there was a part of my personality that enjoys that kind of professional pressure.

After earning that first instructor credential, I went on to quite a few more. And as my trainer resume grew, I found myself traveling further and further away from my "day job" to accommodate the training needs of other agencies and organizations. By the time I had bumped up against both coasts, I decided that I was finally ready to focus on teaching others. So I left law enforcement to work in the training and consulting realm full-time.

I was lucky. It's been a good fit. Over the years I have trained tens of thousands of people. I have consulted for Fortune 500 companies. I designed the post-9/11 cabin crew training program used by the Transportation Security Administration. For the Department of Homeland Security, I literally wrote the book (actually it was their training manual) on protecting soft targets from terror attacks.

For five years I was a bodyguard to some of the wealthiest and most influential people in the world – billionaires and Hollywood "A-listers."

I appeared on national television and radio and became (at age 46) a professional strongman and have performed feats of strength acknowledged by Ripley's Believe It or Not and Guinness World Records. (Okay, I admit, *that* part of the story even *I* didn't see coming.)

In other words – despite a number of very real and very specific obstacles early on – I found a way to reverse the course of my life and turn it into what I had always dreamed of.

I share these things not to boast – they are simply examples of what is possible when mental toughness is combined with hard work.

What should be of interest to you is that I achieved all this and more using the tools and tactics I am going to share with you in **Mind Boss.**

It doesn't matter whether you want to earn more money, fix your fitness, improve your relationships, or achieve any other *realistic yet challenging goal* – the protocols you will learn in **Mind Boss** can get you there.

All that is required of you is to take ACTION.

Taking action is of critical importance.

Too many people buy self-help books thinking that they hold a "golden ticket" to success – a collection of tricks to attain some future achievement. Yet nothing could be further from the truth.

Success requires getting your mind right and then doing the work.

In **Mind Boss** I share specific techniques that have origins in a wide variety of areas—techniques with roots in law enforcement and military training, sports psychology, hypnosis, the martial arts and neuro-linguistic programming. I have combined them with observations and tips from my own unique life. I have done my best to filter out the technical aspects and make this material as accessible as possible. My intent is for you to "get" the material quickly so that you can implement it as soon as possible.

In addition to a wealth of tips and techniques, **Mind Boss** contains stories. I tell stories when I teach. (Although when teaching SWAT operators or military personnel I don't call them stories; I refer to them as "tactical parables.") As you read them, I trust these stories will bring to life some of the larger concepts that **Mind Boss** is built around.

The simple truth of **Mind Boss** is that it does contain a five-step process that you can use to bring success into your life – provided you are willing to TAKE ACTION.

Without action nothing happens. At all.

CHAPTER 1: PASSION FIRST!

"What we seek we shall find; what we flee from flees from us."
Ralph Waldo Emerson

Passion – The First Tenet of Tough Thinking

It really does not matter what exactly you want to achieve, one thing remains true – if you want success – your journey must begin with PASSION.

There are many misconceptions about success and successful people. There are those who believe that wealthy people do what they do simply "for the money."

Many people think that those who are extremely fit are just "lucky," they've got the "right genes" they can "eat whatever they want and get away with it."

And often people assume that those who excel at music or painting are "talented," or they're just "born that way."

Yet the reality is that these types of opinions really miss the mark. And this kind of thinking leads people (sometimes deliberately) to avoid the hard truth. And this hard truth is that making positive change in your life is **hard work.**

Keeping positive change as a constant in your life is also hard work. And achieving truly amazing goals also requires (wait for it…) **lots** of hard work.

The truth is most wealthy people are incredibly passionate about what they do. They wake up early every day and work more hours than the "average" person. And you are not likely to hear them complaining about doing so.

How can I claim to know this?

The answer is simple. I have spent a considerable amount of time with the very richest men on the planet, accompanying them for hours every day, days on end, in my role as an executive bodyguard.

And in spending time with the most storied of billionaires, I can tell you – these guys work hard. Harder and much longer than the average person with a 9 to 5 job. And the reason why they work so hard, despite already being extremely wealthy, is because they are still passionate about what they do. They truly do love it.

When you are really passionate about something – be it something financial, physical, or whatever else you care to think of – you find ways to make things happen.

So what am I telling you?

That your passion for something is directly related to the success you are likely to attain. You can work hard on things you don't care all that much about. But when you have a real passion for something, you find ways to go beyond what hard work alone can accomplish. Passion unlocks enthusiasm and creativity. It is when you can't stop thinking about something that you really start tapping into all that you're capable of.

You almost always find a way to achieve *any* realistic, yet challenging goal once you become passionate enough about it. On the other hand, even the most modest of goals can become impossible to achieve if you do not engage with those goals on an emotional level. Once you take passion out of the equation, things become a struggle.

Now there is a huge difference between being a little interested in something and being absolutely passionate about something. People get interested in things all the time without ever doing anything about those things. But when someone connects with their passion – that is when amazing things happen. This is when they start achieving things that others might think are impossible.

The point about passion is that passion really is the point. Success (however you define it) *can* be yours – but you first need to get in touch with what you're really passionate about.

You may want to double your income or purchase a vacation home. Those are worthy goals – and you will achieve them much more easily if you are passionate about whatever it is that you spend your days doing.

You may want to transform yourself physically – perhaps you want to lose 10, 20, 30 or more pounds of body fat. Conversely, you may want to put on some weight by adding some muscle to your frame – whatever the case, your success potential is commensurate with your level of passion.

Perhaps you want to invest in yourself and earn an advanced degree. An excellent goal – but you will need to become (and remain) passionate about doing so, because you are going to have to push yourself for several years to get there.

This is the value of passion. **Passion is the first step to becoming excellent at anything**. With passion, achieving goals becomes crystal clear (especially when combined with the rest of the techniques in **Mind Boss**).

My challenge to you right now is to ask yourself:

–   What am I *really* passionate about?

Write your answers to that question down and keep them safe because they will become very relevant when we talk about *planning* in Chapter 3. Why am I asking you to write? Because writing is the *doing* part of thinking. Writing makes our thoughts "real."

As you write or type, don't put a limit on your thoughts. Instead, allow your mind to really explore. Make the conscious decision that this type of self-exploration is an enjoyable process. So enjoy the process as you answer the question "What am I really passionate about?" Aim to write for at least three to five minutes.

If you aren't really passionate about anything right now, that's okay. If this is the case, then simply ask yourself the question:

"What *could* I become really passionate about?"

Once you have completed this exercise, we will move on and address the invisible monster in the room that keeps most people from attaining success.

Fear – The Thing That Holds You Back

Fear. Fear gets in the way of so many things: happiness, contentment, self-acceptance, relationships, and especially success.

Fear can prevent people from getting passionate about something in the first place.

Fear prevents people from acting on their passions and "making things happen."

Yet it does not have to be this way. Fear does not have to hold you back. In the next few sections of this chapter you will learn about what fear really is (it is not what most people think) and what it takes to overcome your fears.

I am going to start with a story – a story that demonstrates how fear can be overcome, no matter how strong the feeling is.

During my childhood I spent much of my time being afraid. Most of the things that I was afraid of were "real." Meaning that they were real things that were part of my young life... illegal drugs in the house, being left alone overnight, of other kids finding out what my life was "really like," or if my violent stepfather would one day actually kill my mother. But I was also afraid of things that were less tangible. Specifically, I had grown up with an inexplicable fear of heights. As a kid I tried to avoid things like large staircases and even certain playground equipment. And I would often dream about falling. Falling from ledges, off of roofs, ladders, and bridges. I never understood why, it was just a part of my personal landscape.

In May of 1974, I had just turned 12 years old when a magazine arrived in our mailbox. The cover photograph frightened me although I wasn't exactly sure what I was looking at. That photo depicted climber/photographer Galen Rowell at almost 1,000 feet up the sheer rock face of Half Dome in California's Yosemite Valley. I simply could not fathom being that high in the air...on purpose. It was one of the scarier things that I'd ever seen. And yet every time I put that magazine down, I found myself picking it back up. Just to look at that photograph.

Inside the magazine was an article authored by Rowell which documented his climb up Half Dome. The article featured more terrifying photographs, including one of another climber in a sleeping sack roped to the sheer rock wall. The idea of a person actually sleeping in a nylon bag staked to a cliff was even scarier to me than the idea of climbing up there in the first place.

One thing to bear in mind is that 40 years ago, rock-climbing was not a mainstream activity. The average person had no idea what it was. There were no trendy outdoor shops, climbing gyms or glossy magazines. Those all came years later. So what I was seeing and reading about in that issue of *National Geographic* was not only scary, it also seemed somewhat mysterious.

At 12, I didn't realize that my fear of heights was unusual. I assumed that everyone was as scared of high places as I was. And that is part of why I was so fascinated by Rowell and his climbing companions. I figured that even though they too were terrified, they still had some compelling reason to haul each other up that vertical wall. So I re-read that article throughout that summer. I memorized every detail of each photograph. I wanted to understand why those three men would do something so absolutely terrifying. Because whatever their reason was, it had to be a powerful one.

At the end of that same summer, I was at a state park that features a hiking trail that winds around numerous limestone rock faces. It was a park not far from where I lived and I had walked along that trail many times before. But on this day, something made me stop. That something was a rock face that was perhaps 20 to 25 feet high. I looked up at it and was immediately afraid. But for some reason I approached the base of that cliff and began to climb. I remember getting stuck several times, and I remember the fear of those specific moments. And then I remember getting to the top. I definitely remember what that felt like. Strangely, I had felt fear the entire way up. But I felt something else too. Something that belonged to me. Something I wanted to experience again.

Within the next year I had managed to find some local rudimentary instruction on rock-climbing. With my limited finances I slowly began to acquire the basic equipment I would need to go up and down a modest rock face. In our corn crib (a smaller version of a barn), using scrap pieces of wood, I fashioned a very crude climbing wall with splinter-filled hand- and foot-holds. After school each day I would climb up and down that wall, or rappel from the rafters, or traverse a fixed rope which spanned the length of the corn crib.

Those early climbing "adventures" allowed me to confront something frightening entirely on my own. I had found climbing on my own and I pursued it on my own. It didn't completely eliminate my fear of heights, but I found that I could manage it. In my case, the good outweighed the bad. And if I focused on the good, the bad was always something I could deal with.

I share this story to highlight the fact that you can overcome fear and act in spite of it. Notice that I say "act in spite of it." Because I still felt some fear when I would go climbing.

In recent years, as I have become more involved in the area of personal coaching, I have had people ask me to "take away" their fear. And while this is understandable, it is not really a desirable outcome. We actually need to be able to experience fear. Fear is the early-warning system that our mind uses to communicate life-saving information to the body. And even if we wanted to banish fear from our lives, to do so would eliminate our humanity. According to psychologists, the only people who do not experience any form of fear are, by definition, psychotic.

Fear is a compelling topic. I have spent quite a few years working in both "scary" occupations and doing "scary" things. Things that prompt the average person to say things like, "You couldn't pay me enough to do that!" or "You'd have to be crazy to do that!" And in addition to doing scary things, I have spent a lot of time working with people to prepare them for "scary" situations. Situations which might have to do with their jobs or simply due to recent circumstances in their personal lives.

I refer to this preparation as fear management training. The term management is a subtle but critical distinction. Note that I did not say fear elimination training. This is because fear is not something to be eliminated. You don't get to banish fear away to a far-off place. And you shouldn't want to. Fear will always be part of your perceptual landscape, as much a constant as sweat, sore feet, or sleepiness.

I have heard some well-meaning "experts" tell people such things as "You must embrace your fears, become one with them..." First off, that's a very vague idea. Secondly, that's a bit like "embracing" a hurt knee. You wouldn't hug your knee to make it better. You would talk to someone you trust to find the best way to recondition your knee and restore its functionality. You wouldn't draw pictures of it, imagine that it has colors, or pretend that you're talking to it.

The idea of "embracing" something elevates it, giving it a disproportionate amount of significance. Fear is not to be elevated; it should simply be acknowledged. While I'm not a psychologist, I know that people are primarily afraid of two things... physical and emotional pain. Just about everything you can think of falls pretty neatly into one of those two categories.

Oddly enough, more people get hung up on avoiding emotional pain than the physical kind. And this is despite the fact that things that cause physical pain are often things that can kill you. But people regularly make risky decisions while avoiding mundane activities which at their worst might make them look foolish. Why do so many people say they are afraid of public speaking? Because the potential for embarrassment, or emotional pain.

Dealing with fear is a real issue. But it's not a mystical process. It should be handled systematically. But just like therapies, medications, and workout regimens, one size doesn't fit all. Different fears require different methods, and there are plenty of reasonable methods out there. For many years my specialty was those fears that are associated with interpersonal violence, and it is serious stuff. It is not to be approached the same way as a fear of spiders. But both examples can be dealt with.

If a lack of education was holding you back, you'd do something about it. You'd study, take classes and earn whatever credential you needed to move forward. Fear should not be treated any differently. Don't hug it, identify it. Quantify what it really is and then make your plan to deal with it. We know that muscles can be strengthened and brain function can be improved. So do the same thing with your courage. Think of it as "limitation elimination."

Mind Boss is about taking action in spite of your fear. Unfortunately, many people are operating from a "fear-control" perspective, allowing their fear to control the amount of satisfaction they experience in their lives.

While I experienced fear when I began rock-climbing, I simply found how to deal with it and overcome it. One of the primary reasons I was able to act in spite of fear was because I created goals that were **big** enough and **important** enough to me that they became bigger than the fear.

Always remember – *if your goal is bigger and more powerful to you than the fear associated with it – you can push forward and find a way to make your goal a reality.* However, if the fear is more powerful than the goal – (as it is for most people) you likely will not take any action and the fear will win. It will stop you dead in your tracks.

It all comes back to getting passionate about something. It's that passion and desire to do something that creates the mind-set of *"I will succeed no matter what."* That is the mind-set of a winner.

That said – there are some other techniques for overcoming fear that you will learn later in this chapter.

First though, let's answer the question...

What Is Fear?

Before I can teach you skills to effectively overcome fear, you have to really understand *what* fear is. And the more one can understand and demystify fear, the less fearful you will be.

To begin with, we will break fear into three separate categories:

i.   A feeling of anxiety caused by the presence or imminence of danger.

ii. A feeling or reason for apprehension: *a fear of looking foolish.*

iii. A condition marked by this feeling: *living in fear.*

Now let's take a more detailed look at each of these...

Definition 1: A feeling of anxiety caused by the presence or imminence of danger

In this case the feeling of fear arises because of a potential or actual threat. In this scenario, fear can motivate you to make very quick and positive decisions *that can save your life.*

Imagine a situation where you are walking alone at night, through an unfamiliar neighborhood – in a part of town known for its crime rate. Yes, I know, you're much too smart to be doing that sort of thing. But for the moment, mentally put yourself into that situation. Really see the details and above all, imagine what the situation would feel like.

A couple hundred yards ahead you see a group of people standing around on a street corner. They look fairly young and they're making a lot of noise.

You do not know whether or not they pose any *actual* danger to you, but you feel fear because of the <u>potential</u> danger. You also know that if they did become violent, you would be in a poor position to defend yourself because there are many of them and only one of you. Plus, there is nobody else around due to the time of night. With all of these factors combined, you feel fear.

The optimal outcome based upon your perceptions would be a quick detour to your destination and bypass the potential threat entirely. You would never know whether or not that decision maintained your well-being, but you stack the odds in your favor when you pay attention to what's going on around you and make decisions accordingly.

Now imagine another scenario. You are walking down an alleyway you've used as a shortcut. There is only you in the alleyway, or so you think, but then a man suddenly appears from a doorway some ten yards in front of you.

The man doesn't look friendly, he appears to be drunk, and he is muttering to himself as he approaches you. As the man gets within a few yards of you – he suddenly pulls a knife!

You instantly react by turning around and running as fast as you can. Fortunately, the man cannot keep up with you and you get back to the main road street safe and unhurt - having avoided a confrontation.

In this scenario the feeling of fear was based on *a very real physical threat.* When somebody brandishes a knife, you must assume that they are willing to use it.

Your fear caused you to make a quick and very sensible decision – to turn around and run as fast as you could. That decision quite possibly saved your life.

So the question is…

Was the feeling of fear a *bad* thing in either of these two scenarios? It clearly was *not.* It was a feeling that in all likelihood caused you to react in such a way that you avoided bodily harm.

These examples highlight the true purpose of fear – as a *protective mechanism.* You feel fear…it acts as a warning sign…you make a decision…and hopefully that decision takes you away from potential or actual danger.

But this *isn't* where most people are experiencing fear most of the time. Let's consider the second definition of fear…

Definition 2: A feeling or reason for apprehension: *a fear of looking foolish*...

In this scenario fear is a feeling of apprehension. A fear of looking *foolish* is a great example of this kind of fear. The interesting thing is that there is no real danger associated with this type of fear. Yet this is where so many people feel fear and become immobilized by it.

A common example of this is the fear associated with speaking in public. According to a number of studies, a majority of people have stated that they fear public speaking more than they fear dying. For those of us who speak for a living, this is a bit difficult to understand.

Public speaking tends to be a complex phobia comprised of several others; such as fear of open spaces or crowds (agoraphobia), fear of people (anthropophobia), fear of failure (atychiphobia), fear of ridicule (catagelophobia), fear of confined spaces (claustrophobia), and fear of social evaluation (sociophobia).

To overcome the fear of public speaking, it is important to understand some basics about human communication itself...

In the 1960s, a UCLA communications professor named Albert Mehrabian concluded that interpersonal communication occurs via three primary channels. And according to Mehrabian, each one of these channels has a relatively constant level of impact on the message that is perceived by an audience. These include the actual words we use; voice qualities such as tone, inflection, and emphasis; and the non-verbal communication that accompanies the words. (What is commonly referred to as body-language).

And though it may seem counterintuitive, the specific words we use actually have the least overall impact in terms of the message our audience perceives. Words actually account for approximately 10% of message meaning. In contrast, voice qualities provide almost 40% of message meaning while non-verbal communication provides over 50%.

So why is this important to know for those who are afraid of speaking in public?

Here's why...

Most people get stuck on the idea that whenever you address an audience you must know "the perfect thing to say." But this is not actually the case. As these percentages indicate, it truly is not *what* you say. Rather, it is *how* you say it.

So if you have ever suffered from a fear of public speaking, take some comfort in the fact that you don't need to wait until you have found the perfect words to share. You do, however, need to convey your message with power , certainty and conviction. In other words, you simply need to speak honestly and authentically. A little passion in your voice and your actions helps too. Your audience will respond to what you have to say when your words, voice qualities and body language all support each other.

The fear of public speaking really illuminates the way that most people experience fear. Again, there is no physical danger associated with public speaking. Most people are instead feeling fears *associated* with public speaking. Things like...

— Fear of failure

and...

— Fear of social evaluation and ridicule

These are fears based on EGO.

If you suddenly had to evacuate a tall office building by means of a rickety fire escape, that's legitimate fear. You are in physical danger. And that fear is a sign to do something and do it quickly because your life is in peril.

If however, you suddenly feel fear because you have to give a fifteen-minute presentation in front of your work colleagues – this is fear based on your ego. There is no physical danger present; you are simply feeling fearful because you are afraid that you might look unprepared, appear nervous, or simply come off as less than perfect.

But here's the thing...

Let's say that you did appear less than fully prepared or you looked nervous while giving a fifteen-minute presentation... is that *really* such a big deal?

Not really. Well, it's certainly not comparable to staring down a rattlesnake or having to leap over quicksand.

So is fear a compelling reason to avoid public speaking? I would say no. Ego-based fear is simply a dragon that needs slaying.

While these first two types of fear are understandable to almost everyone, the third type doesn't just get in the way of success, it gets in the way of living your life…

Definition 3: An ongoing condition marked by this feeling : *living in fear…*

The person who "lives in fear" is apt to see the world as a big, scary place. And their ensuing fears can begin to dictate their daily life. Needless to say, this is both an unpleasant and unproductive way to live.

As an example, consider those people who obsess about an imagined imminent governmental collapse. They see society as they know it breaking down. The hypothetical result would be some sort of desolate, apocalyptic science fiction-like wasteland. So following their belief that "the end of the world is coming," they devote their days to preparing for the end.

Think about what living that kind of life would be like.

These people spend all their time learning how to decontaminate themselves from chemical attacks, how to shelter themselves from radioactive fallout and they practice military-style tactics to potentially use against...well, they're not really sure who.

This is an example of allowing fear to dictate your life. It is also an example of how people can confuse being busy with being productive. And while these people are taking a lot of action and doing a lot of things, what do they ultimately accomplish? Are they making the world a better place? Are they adding to the quality of their own lives? The answer is no. What they are doing is keeping themselves so busy that they never have to confront just how afraid they are.

What I want you to be able to do is recognize fear and do what you want to anyway. If you feel fear because of a threat to your life – good. This just means that you're ready to react quickly in order to avoid harm.

If, however, you feel fear because of a threat to your ego (which is where so many people feel fear much of the time), you need to be able to recognize this for what it is and begin to work past it.

I can assure you that every successful person feels fear, in the same way that unsuccessful people do. The difference is that successful people have learned to overcome it and push forward in spite of it – whereas unsuccessful people tend to let fear stop them dead in their tracks.

The Three Reactions to Fear

You have probably heard the expression: "Fight or Flight."

"Fight or Flight" refers to the two reactions most people associate with fear. An example of *fight* is punching someone who tries to attack you. An example of *flight* is running away from someone who tries to attack you.

Simple enough, right? However, things get a little more interesting when you consider the third reaction to fear – the one that most people are unaware of.

The third reaction to fear is to **FREEZE**. This "freezing" is essentially an inability to process a sudden, unexpected amount of stimuli. And to "freeze" in the face of danger is actually common.

When someone freezes in response to fear, it means that they literally do nothing. I have a story that highlights the freeze response, and how freezing, in certain circumstances, could be the last thing your ever do. It's a story that goes back to when I was literally a brand-new police officer. It was a period of time when I learned many valuable lessons from the inevitable mistakes associated with inexperience....

It was an early Wednesday morning as I stood next to my patrol car. I was refueling it in preparation to take it back to the station. It was just after 6:00 a.m. I had worked all night long and I was tired. I was not in a peak state and I certainly was not thinking about having to deal with anything serious in the remaining 20 or so minutes of my shift. And I was still new enough that I didn't have a lot of experience with that whole idea of things happening when you least expect them.

So in my mind – my shift was basically finished, with nothing left to do but put my squad car in the garage and close out my paperwork. Mentally, I had already "clocked out" from my shift and was not prepared for what would happen next....

Suddenly, I got a call from the station. It was a "suicide in progress" and the subject in question was armed with a knife.

Thanks to a sudden rush of adrenaline, I was able to shake off my fatigue and transition to a state of amplified awareness. I put my foot on the gas and rushed to the address.

When I arrived, I found several people outside, including a young woman (who I would later find out was the subject's girlfriend) holding a baby. As soon as I exited the car, she pointed at the house and screamed: "He's in the basement. He has a knife. He's crazy!"

Needless to say, I'd become wide-awake at this point.

I went into the house and peered down the stairway into the pitch-black basement. I called the guy's name and tried to sound reassuring. I had hoped that I could get him to come to me.

I had also expected that anyone who was "crazy" would be loud, moving around, and easy to find. But this guy was none of those things. So I started navigating my way down the basement stairs to begin the tense work of finding someone whose distinguishing characteristics were being crazy and armed with a knife. As I hit the floor of the basement, I turned on my flashlight and began searching.

I could not see him.

The basement was divided into several rooms and I methodically moved forward, looking and listening for any sign of this guy. It had occurred to me that the silence might have been due to the fact that he had proceeded with this plan to kill himself and that I might very well come across him lying on the floor, possibly dead or dying.

As I turned another corner, he was suddenly standing right in front of me. He may have been there the whole time. But now he stood no more than four feet away, illuminated by my flashlight. And that's when I noticed that I was sort of frozen. Because my eyes had settled upon the base of his neck and stayed there. Running across the front of his neck was a jagged wound where he had tried to slit his own throat.

And that was my mistake. I had become perceptually frozen, mentally captivated by what I was looking at.

As I stood, momentarily hypnotized by this very grim, very painful-looking wound I did not do what I should have done – which was to immediately check his hands to see if he was holding the knife or any other weapon which he could use against me or to inflict further damage upon himself.

I had become FROZEN while gazing at this gruesome and unexpected wound.

Now, this was for a fraction of a second, but during that brief moment I was completely absorbed by what I saw and overtaken by the mental dialogue that accompanied it.

"Why would he do such a thing? Is it as painful as it looks? Why isn't there more blood?"

So not only was I frozen, I was also asking myself rhetorical questions when I was supposed to be taking action.

After what might have been just a half-second (but felt like much, much longer) I regained my senses, glanced down, and saw that the guy did indeed have a weapon in his hands – a very serious-looking knife. And when he saw that I had seen his knife, the fight was on.

I went for the knife, he went for me, and the next minute or so was a blur. Luckily I was able to disarm him, restrain him, get him medical help, and fortunately he survived and I walked away unharmed.

It is moments like this when a certain phrase comes to mind. And that phrase is "Never confuse good luck with good planning."

In this instance I had simply been lucky. And later in the book when we get to the topic of analyzing feedback, it will be imperative to understand the difference between good luck and good planning. Because as soon as I saw the man in the basement, I *should* have immediately created some distance and monitored his hands for any weapons. Instead, I fixated on his wound and froze. And this could have led to me getting cut or even stabbed.

Freezing happens. In the story I just shared, this freezing had accompanied the presence of potential danger. But so much of the time it does not. Most people freeze in response to the fear they feel most often – fear based on the ego and potential harm to their self-esteem.

Anytime where you find yourself in a situation that you are not happy with and you still do nothing about it – that is an example of freezing. And I firmly believe that freezing in response to those things which are uncomfortable or scary becomes easier over time. This is because the more we let fear freeze us into inaction, the more likely we are to repeat that behavior in the future.

Perhaps you're familiar with the term "conditioned response." What I am describing is an example of training or "conditioning" yourself to respond to difficult situations by doing nothing…taking no action, making no decisions, and waiting for the situation (often an opportunity) to pass you by.

How to Overcome Fear

One effective way to overcome fear is through what psychologists refer to as exposure therapy.

Here is an example of how it can work….

As a young child I was so afraid of heights that I could not ride in a car over a bridge without closing my eyes. Yet I became an ardent rock-climber by age 13.

I was able to triumph over trepidation through repeated *exposure*. I systematically began attacking rock faces and just kept at. Over time I was able to tackle longer and steeper stretches of rock in my pursuit to get better. And by "better," I don't mean that I was specifically interested in becoming a more skillful climber. For me "better" had to do with what I experienced during the process of climbing. Climbing was making *me* better.

The more I climbed and the more I realized that I could do so without getting hurt, the more I was able to manage my fear of heights. Simply put, the fear which had captivated me for years was never based on actual danger. It had not been the result of *doing* anything. Instead, it had been a product of *feeling* like I couldn't do anything…a feeling that had followed me around, dragging down any inclinations I may have had to engage with life in an adventurous way.

This "exposure" approach worked for me much the same way years later when I progressed to jumping out of airplanes. And the first time *was* scary, but as I did it over and over again, the feelings associated with jumping changed. And for me, it ultimately became something that I enjoyed doing. So much so, that I would seek out opportunities to get in on as many jumps as I was able. The Army has a term for those who volunteer to jump with other units, often as a last-minute seat-filler, and I became what is referred to as a "straphanger."

But there is one more point to jumping out of airplanes that is relevant to anyone who aspires to master their fear. And that point is this...while I was in the Army, I met more than a few guys who confided to me that they hated to jump. They found jumping scary and unpleasant and they dreaded every jump that they were assigned to make.

So the inevitable question is why would you volunteer for service in the 82d Airborne Division if you feared heights and hated jumping from airplanes? We've actually already answered this question. It goes back to the point I made about your goal. If it is bigger and more powerful to you than the fear associated with it, you will find a way to make your goal a reality.

These young men hated jumping. They hated standing in the open doorway of an aircraft, often during the hours of complete darkness, knowing that ground was somewhere far below them. But they had also felt something else stronger than that fear. And that something was the pride of serving in an elite unit. Of being part of something important. Something larger than themselves. That is what allowed them to manage their fears and do something which represented significance to them.

Exposure, combined with a strong *goal orientation*, is a very effective way to mitigate FEAR.

Here's an important point...

When it comes to exposure, generally speaking – the more the better.

For instance, let's say you have a fear of public speaking and you want to get to the point where public speaking no longer bothers you. Do you think you will get faster results if you do one public speaking event a year, or one a week?

The answer is obvious, *right?*

You'd do one a week.

If you are going to successfully use exposure as a tool to overcome fear, the exposure needs to be frequently and consistently applied.

Here's another example of how exposure can overcome fear. As a child, I grew up watching my stepfather subject my mother to horrific beatings. It terrified me and fed into a sense of helplessness that took a long time to shake. As young as eight, I had become very attuned to the angry words which would precede the explosions of physical violence so I would try to get as far away from the situation as I could.

When I was 10 years old, we moved to the country. And in this new setting I frequently chose to sleep outdoors in one of our old wooden farm sheds. Sometimes I would just sleep in a sleeping bag out in the yard. I wasn't forced to do this. I simply found that being outside, on my own, was preferable to being around the endless alcohol-fueled violence which would play out indoors... violence which terrified me.

And somehow, years later, that same small, frightened kid became one of the most sought-after experts in the arena of violence management training and a protector of the world's wealthiest executives. And while it certainly didn't happen overnight, as a result of consistent exposure it did happen. Through my police field experiences, numerous training courses, exhaustive academic research and a burning desire to help others succeed in this area, I was repeatedly "exposed" to violence. All facets of it, again and again. And this self-directed study ultimately yielded a positive outcome from the altogether negative phenomena of violence.

All of this goes back to the idea of getting passionate about something. In the same way that I was passionate about transcending the circumstances of my young life, **you** need to find those things which will propel **you** forward. Forward past your fears and past the inevitable obstacles.

So when you look inward and contemplate the feelings that threaten to freeze you in place, ask yourself the following question:

"Is this fear I am feeling a threat to my well-being, or is it simply a threat to my ego?"

If the answer is that you're feeling an "ego-based threat," then it's time to find a way to push past the fear and do the thing that is making you afraid *anyway*. To act in this way, you have to...

Become Courageous

Successful people display courage. Not necessarily the kind of courage displayed by warriors going into battle, but if you start to study winners, you'll consistently find examples of courage.

Here is what I mean…

When someone experiences fear based on the ego, it is usually due to two things:

i.   Fear of Accountability
ii. Fear of Visibility

I believe that it is these fears which most often hold people back and stops them from achieving what they want.

Some examples will make what I am saying very clear…

Imagine a person who has done the same job for 15 years and is essentially unhappy with it. They would like to earn more money and they would like to experience more enjoyment while doing so.

The good news: This person is qualified to do better things. Much better things.

The bad news: This person never does take any action and they carry on doing the same job that they dislike.

So why didn't this person take any action?

The likely answer is that they are afraid of both the accountability and visibility associated with doing so.

If they go for a job interview they will have to tell people about it.

That interview becomes a **visible** step. People now know about it.

This interview will also have an outcome. An outcome that they are **accountable** for.

And of course the outcome of this job interview will be **visible**... to their current boss and co-workers, to their friends, family, and so on. So instead of simply pursuing a job they want, they let opportunities pass by, just to avoid the visibility and accountability associated with taking proactive steps. After all, there is no scrutiny when chances are not taken.

This is a prime example of someone letting the fear of accountability and visibility prevent them from taking action and making positive changes in their lives.

To overcome circumstances like these, you must find the COURAGE necessary to take action in spite of your fear.

Now if you've made it to this point but you just don't *feel* courageous yet, that's okay. *Feeling* courageous is not nearly as important as *acting* courageous. And to act courageous, all you have to do is that thing that scares you. It doesn't mean that you're not still scared, it just means that you are going to do that thing anyway.

This is huge. Like anything else, exhibiting courage is a trained skill. The more often it is practiced, the easier it becomes.

In other words, do not let the fears of accountability and visibility hold you back as they do so many people.

Remember: Success in any arena takes courage.

It takes courage to pursue a job promotion or start a new business.

It takes courage to change your eating habits and lose weight.

It takes courage to go back to school and sit in classes where the other students are more advanced than you.

But the results are worth it, even if you're not successful every time. Let the act of deliberately doing something that makes you uncomfortable be its own reward. Overcoming fear feels good. In contrast, allowing the fear of accountability, visibility, or failure to prevent you from taking action never feels good.

Get Passionate About Something

Mind Boss is a 5-step process for achieving what you want. And I emphatically believe that you can achieve amazing things if you marshal sufficient amounts of passion.

With abundant passion – you can overcome any amount of fear, earn more money than you can imagine, build the kind of body that people admire, and do, have, and become anything you desire.

If you want to feel amazing and make your life something extraordinary – you have to be passionate. Make it your mission to spend as much of your time as possible doing things that you are really passionate about, because that is what successful people do.

Exercise

It's one thing to just tell yourself to relax during those times when you're experiencing stress or fear. But it's much easier when you have a specific technique to do just that. The exercise I am about to share with you is a very simple way to center yourself and feel a greater sense of control when faced with feelings of fear.

I first learned this in my law enforcement days and have used the technique many times. I've performed it while driving at high speeds when en route to crimes in progress, before drug-lab raids, and any other time when I knew I had to keep my emotions under control.

Consider this exercise a tool that can help you to act in the face of fear.

Here's how it works…

- Sit comfortably or lie down

- Close your eyes if appropriate or safe to do so

- Breathe in through your nose for a 4 count

- Hold the air in for a 4 count

—   Breathe out gently through your mouth for a 4 count

—   Pause for a 4 count

—   Repeat this process for 2-3 minutes

This is a very simple exercise, but the results are powerful. Try it the next time you feel fear, stress, or anytime you want to feel more "in control."

The most important performance point of this exercise is to ensure that you are filling your abdomen with air, as opposed to your chest. This is called diaphragmatic breathing.

If you're not sure you're doing it correctly, stand in front of a mirror. Place your hands on your abdomen and observe yourself as you breathe.

What do you notice?

Do your shoulders rise and fall as you breathe or do you feel your abdomen moving in and out?

If your shoulders rise and fall, then you are still "chest" breathing. Keep working until you can consistently observe and feel your abdomen filling with air as you inhale. Once you can visually confirm that your shoulders remain still as the abdomen moves in and out – you will be breathing correctly.

Diaphragmatic breathing is reputed to have many benefits. These include reductions in blood pressure, strengthening of the abdominal and intestinal muscles and improved oxygen uptake in the bloodstream.

Three Suggestions

i. Start putting this technique to use. A perfect time to practice is as you lie in bed preparing to go to sleep for the night. You should find that not only will the rhythmic breathing relax you, concentrating on the process and the associated counting will help eliminate the random distracting thoughts that keep many people awake at night.

ii. Learn to recognize the difference between danger to your physical well-being (*"real" fear*) and fears based merely on accountability or visibility (*"self-generated" fear*). Most people are surprised to discover just how many of the fears that they experience are actually obstacles of their own creation. It's time to stop letting these self-generated fears hold you back.

iii. If you want to make your life truly exceptional, you need to look at things holistically. Everything you do impacts everything else you do. Commit to becoming passionate about your physical self, your job/career and your relationships. When you bring passion to these areas – your physical self, your job/career, and your relationships – you will begin to improve the quality of your life in ways you might have not thought possible.

CHAPTER 2: PREPARE WELL

"You either know what you can do; or you just
think you know...."
Guy Savelli

Preparation – The Second Tenet of Tough Thinking

To make positive changes in any area of your life – whether those changes have to do with your health and physical body, your job or career, your relationships, or anything else you care to name – you have to be *prepared* to do so. You have to be ready to TAKE ACTION and you have to have a clear understanding of where you are now and where you want to be.

One of the biggest things that can hold people back is the idea that WHAT they are doing now is WHO they really are. This is an example of limited thinking. And it is this kind of limited thinking that keeps most people right where they are – and a long way from where they want to be.

Consider the case of somebody working the fryer at a fast-food restaurant. They flip burgers and make fries all day, earning a nominal wage and are not likely to be very satisfied with their job.

People in these situations often allow themselves to start thinking that **what** they are doing (making burgers and fries) is **who** they really are. And unfortunately, if they continue thinking this way, this self-belief will ultimately become a very limiting, self-fulfilling prophecy.

Yet that is not the true reality of the situation. (After all, I too used to work at a fast-food restaurant way back in high school.)

The reality of the situation is that this person could do any number of more mentally stimulating and financially rewarding jobs than making hamburgers and french fries. But to do so, they must first be open to the idea. They must understand that massive change *is* possible, providing it is realistic*.

*It's important to understand what I mean when I say "realistic." For example, if you decide one day that you want to become the President of the United States of America and that nothing less than becoming the president will make you happy, you will almost certainly find yourself unhappy, because this particular goal is not a realistic one.

Now, if you came from the right kind of family, with the right type of legacy relationships and current social connections, have the right education, enough money and mix with the right people – you *may* have a chance of one day *running* for president. But it's still a very small chance… then you have to <u>win</u> the presidential campaign. So, for more than 99% of people, trying to become president of the USA is a goal that is going to make them unhappy because it is realistically unattainable.

Now, if you came to me and told me that you currently earn $40,000 and you would like to increase your income to $60,000 within the next 18 months, I'd be ready to help you work out just HOW you were going to do it. You see, that goal is far more realistic, as well as challenging.

Likewise, let's say you just started studying the martial art of karate. You have been practicing for a few weeks and so far only have your white belt. You tell me that you are willing to practice daily for at least an hour and want to get to your black belt within three years.

Again, I'd encourage you to pursue this goal. Is it *easy*? No. Is it *challenging*? Yes. But above all, it is **achievable** with hard work.

This is what I mean when I say *realistic*. And by the way – people tend to be very conservative with their goals. You need to balance reality with reward. So go large. Stop telling yourself that what you are doing now is all you'll ever be able to do, because that is not the case. You can always *do* more and *become* more than you are right now. So right now, start planning to become a better version of yourself.

The key point is that to achieve whatever it is that YOU desire, you must **prepare** yourself for success. And a massive part of the preparation process is....

Getting In Touch With Reality

I often refer to our current generation in the Western world as "the self-esteem generation." People have been spoon-fed a false sense of self-worth based on the nebulous idea that they are "special." This "specialness" is not an award of achievement; instead it's a vague attribute that gets passed out like a locker room towel.

Now this is all done with the best of intentions–to make folks feel good about themselves. And I'm not saying that the people in your life shouldn't feel special because they are special to *you*, because they should. But if *you* aspire to be regarded as special to more than just a handful of people, then you need to go out and actually do something. Work hard, serve others, innovate, but DO something.

Some will disagree with my premise. To them, this sounds like too much "tough love." And therein lies the problem. It isn't fashionable these days to confront hard truths. As a result, I don't think that as a society we have a collective grasp of reality.

There are four prevailing factors which lead me to say this...

i.   **Artificial Destiny.**
     It has become fashionable for youngsters to be told that they have the potential to do things that they cannot...

the earlier example of becoming president of the United States being a prime example.

Kids are told that "You can be whatever you want to be" so long as "You just set your mind to it." But these are empty words. They are the language of non-specific pleasantness. It's fluffy verbiage that serves only to undermine the recipient once they have to navigate their lives in the real world.

Wherever and whenever you are looking to create positive changes in your life, those changes will need to have a basis in reality.

Let's go back to our martial arts analogy. Imagine in this case that you are now 50 years old and have just begun studying karate. And let's say that you told me you wanted your black belt within three years. In this case I'd say "Go for it" because it's entirely doable with consistent practice.

However, if you were 50 years old and you told me you wanted to become a world champion boxer, I'd suggest a quick reality check. I'd tell you to start asking some specific questions – questions like: "What is the average age of world champion boxers and at what age do most boxers retire?"

When you ask thoughtful and objective questions – you get

practical answers and you can quickly work out whether or not you are operating within the realm of reality and *real* possibility.

So by all means set yourself big, inspirational goals... goals that keep you up late at night and get you up early in the morning...goals that most people will think are impossible. But just make sure you always operate from a place of reality. Leave the fantasy stuff for Hollywood.

ii. False Sense of Entitlement

Many people have what is best described as a false sense of entitlement. Here's how this works:

"You're a good person. You *deserve* nice a nice house... a good job... and everything else you desire...."

Really? Well let me offer a dissenting opinion:

No. You. Don't.

Statements like that are simply wrong. They're no truer than saying that children who are born into poverty and sickness deserve those things.

False expectations are ultimately destructive. They lay the foundation for creating lazy people who are not prepared to dig deep and make things happen; people who moan and complain because they feel like they "deserve" things they don't have.

Here is the reality of the situation.

You are entitled to absolutely *anything* you desire, so long as you are willing to roll up your sleeves and work both hard and *smart* to get it. And as long as whatever you desire is within the realms of the law and doesn't bring harm to anybody else.

You can have the body of your dreams – provided you are willing to eat a sound diet at least 90% of the time, exercise. and not abuse yourself with harmful substances.

You can have plenty of money, providing you are willing to obtain the necessary schooling to earn the kind of degree it takes to secure a lucrative job, OR if you are prepared to start your own business. Short of resorting to a life of crime (not recommended) you cannot expect to have a lot of money without working hard and taking **real action** to make it happen.

You can have a wonderful, nurturing relationship with your partner, but not without some effort. For a relationship to be successful in the long run, you should expect to do some work on your communication skills and in particular, your negotiation skills. You need to learn the art of compromise, how to "give and take."

Here's the bottom line…

You are not entitled to anything simply because you are

you. Yet this is how many people now spend their days – angry at the world because they feel like it owes them things that they have not actually earned.

You are entitled to anything you are prepared to make happen. It all comes back to **taking positive action**. That's what winners do.

iii. Lack of Accountability

Everybody loves telling people about their *successes*. Yet few people are prepared to stand up and say:

"You know what? I completely messed up this time."

Most people are looking to blame someone else. We have become a society where we are always looking for a scapegoat – somebody else to take the fall.

But successful people are always prepared to say "That was *my* fault." And if you want to become more successful and achieve anything you want and desire – you have to be prepared to do the same. You have to be willing to be accountable for your actions, both good and bad. To do anything less is to operate outside of reality.

A recent example of lack of accountability run amok would be the revelations concerning Lance Armstrong, the seven-time winner of the world's most grueling cycling event, the Tour De France.

For years, Lance Armstrong's unprecedented success in this event has been the subject of much speculation. There have been endless accusations that Armstrong was using performance-enhancing drugs (PEDS) when he won his Tour De France titles. But the response from Team Armstrong to these many charges was a consistent and defiant "No." And for years, the general public accepted Armstrong's claims of innocence. This fed into Armstrong's popularity as both an athlete and a cancer survivor, which led to wave after wave of lucrative endorsements.

Then things changed for Lance Armstrong when he was stripped of his Tour De France titles as a result of the findings by the United States Anti-Doping Agency. And as befits a fallen celebrity, he subsequently appeared on Oprah Winfrey's television show to finally admit, after years of vigorous denials, that he had, in fact, used PEDS.

In other words, he finally admitted that he had cheated.

As a result of his admission, many people have gone from loving Lance, supporting his charity, and wearing his Live Strong wristbands, to hating him.

Now it should not be construed that Lance Armstrong was the only Tour De France athlete who ever participated in "blood-doping." In fact, numerous top-placing cyclists have also been implicated in recent years. But Armstrong had stood alone in terms of the magnitude of his fame and his accomplishments.

But the cheating was not the worst of it; it was just part of a bigger picture. People who had worked behind the scenes and had been willing (despite threats to their livelihoods) to speak the truth about Armstrong's use of PEDs had been systematically harassed, sued, and ostracized from competitive cycling. This campaign of intimidation was carried out by Armstrong's organization and often by Armstrong himself.

So where was the accountability in all of this? Certainly most of us can understand how the world of competitive sports creates pressure for an athlete to use any available means to win. But it's much harder to understand how someone who, while cheating, can simultaneously feel justified in destroying others whose only transgressions were to speak the truth.

So what does all this have to do with "getting in touch with reality"? Plenty. When you lose touch with reality, you can start feeling **entitled** to things. And feeling entitled to something is far different from *earning* something.

Armstrong's actions were emblematic of someone who felt that they could flout the rules. That is an entitlement mindset in action. Successful people know that they have to "earn" their success every day. So accountability is not just an efficiency-of-effort issue; it's a character issue, too.

To become truly successful, achieve anything you want, and to be able to look at yourself in the mirror and know that you are a person of integrity, you have to be prepared to be hold yourself accountable for one hundred percent of your actions: the good, the bad, and the ugly.

Any person who is not willing to be face up to the consequences of their words and deeds is ultimately not willing to be "real." They are not being real with others and not being real with themselves. So strive for transparency. You will be amazed how much harder you work and productive you become once you are completely open in all that you do. This is what is meant behind that old expression "honest effort."

iv. **No Coping Skills**

When things are going well, it is easy to be the fun-loving, happy-go-lucky person who walks around with a smile on their face.

Yet the reality is that things do not always go well. And how well you deal with the bad times actually has a lot more to do with your own potential success than how you deal with the good times.

Consider this...

When someone gets a pay raise at work, this is an easy and pleasant development to deal with—a celebratory dinner, a few glasses of wine with friends, and so on. Sounds pretty good, right?

But what about when something bad happens? What are the results when someone loses their job, or their partner leaves them, or they break a leg? How do they deal with *that*?

Sadly, many people do not have the kinds of coping skills they need to overcome and push past the bad or even "not-so-bad" circumstances that happen to them.

Attaining success isn't easy. There are always setbacks, which is why serious success requires real-world coping skills...the kind that equip you to deal with anything life throws your way – especially when it's not something you wanted.

You will need to stay grounded in reality, see the situation for what it is (as something that you *can* deal with because there is *always* a way), and then develop your plan for how to move past it.

Let's re-cap:

To be successful...

– Avoid "artificial destiny syndrome." Say "YES" to challenging goals that are *realistic*, and say "NO" to allowing yourself to be absorbed into the realm of fantasy. (Like those people who base their financial future on attempts to win the lottery.)

—   Avoid "false sense of entitlement syndrome." Get clear on the fact that just because you are YOU, this does not give you an inherent right to the things that you desire. You have to earn what you want through hard and *smart* work – something many people simply aren't prepared to engage in, a fact which is ultimately reflected in their *lack* of success.

—   Be prepared to be accountable for ALL of your actions, both the successes and the mistakes. This is an attribute that tough people have. When you do something well, it's okay to give yourself a pat on the back. Celebrate the good and remember those moments. Conversely, when something you do doesn't turn out so well, be equally prepared to say "That was my mistake." Then figure out how to make sure that same mistake doesn't happen again.

    People who acknowledge only their successes and aren't prepared to authentically address their failures are like gamblers who talk only about their wins. They gradually move further and further from reality.

—   Develop coping skills so that you can handle things when circumstances don't go to plan. This is something successful people have to do because it happens to them so often.

Avoid at all costs those situations where after one thing goes wrong, depression sets in and you then allow multiple, yet unrelated areas of your life to go "downhill." I have seen too many people do this. Once you go down this road, it can be very hard to find your way back up.

While we are discussing reality, here is another key point. Your feelings can actually be that thing that leads you astray, putting you at odds with reality. In fact, your feelings will often lie to you and misguide you.

This happens all kinds of ways. Remember fear? We talked a lot about fear in the previous chapter. So we remember that fear is notorious for generating self-limiting beliefs.

Here's an example. In 2005, my wife Tammie had been searching for something new to do. She had previously spent many years raising our four children. She had run a home-based business so that she could manage her work schedule and still be the proverbial ultra-involved "supermom."

But she was now at a point in her life where she could start thinking about what she *wanted* to do rather than what she felt she *had* to do. And then one day she heard a radio commercial that she felt was speaking directly to her when she heard the words "*You* can be a helicopter pilot."

She immediately phoned me at work to tell me that she had finally figured out what she wanted to do, that she wanted to be a helicopter pilot. And as great as I thought that was, I did point out that she had never even *ridden* in a helicopter before. But undeterred, she began flight training a short time later.

Now here's the point. Tammie had something that she really wanted to do. She had a real sense of purpose for it. But, she still had fear. She first felt fear when she initially signed up. She was a good deal older than the 20-somethings in her class and her fear told her she was too old to do something like this.

She was also a woman among many men and her fear told her that she didn't fit in a male-dominated profession. When she began the initial ground training she found the material to be extremely technical and unlike anything she had ever studied before. So there were times when her fear told her that she would never pass her ground classes.

Then Tammie began the actual flight training and she found that she was extremely susceptible to motion sickness. She came home every day feeling very ill. Her fear tried to convince her that she had made a huge mistake in signing on for the training and that she was not physically suited to fly.

Then there solo flights, night fights, and cross-country flights. All of this flying provided numerous opportunities for her to feel fear. And in particular, there was emergency procedures training.

This is when you simulate engine failure by cutting the power. To survive engine failure, you must "auto-rotate" to the ground.

This is where the air moving up through the blades causes the blades to keep turning as the pilot attempts to make a controlled drop to the ground. So Tammie had to master this as well. And there was fear.

The irony in this situation is that despite all of the different times that she had experienced fear, all the points along the way where her feelings told her that she didn't have it in her and that she should quit like so many of her other classmates, those feelings were LIES.

Because in **reality** she was becoming an exceptional pilot. In fact, she was leading her classmates in terms of performance. This is an essential point, so here it is again... her feelings had been **lying** to her. Over and over again.

If you want to be successful, you have to maintain a strong grasp on reality and you have to realize that your feelings are not always an accurate barometer of what is true.

Quick Tip: It is often not a good idea to act impulsively and in the heat of the moment when you have negative feelings. Instead, take a step back from the situation, use the deep breathing exercise from Chapter 1 to relax yourself and lessen the stress you may feeling. Then try to determine what the true reality of the situation actually is. HINT: The way to arrive at reality in any situation is by asking yourself objective, fact-based questions. Avoid emotion-based questions like "Why do these things always happen to me?" That sort of inner dialogue doesn't lead to solutions, it just drags you further down.

Another part of the "reality puzzle" that you need to respect is that success rarely happens overnight. In other words....

Don't Rush

People try to rush success and achievement all the time and it rarely works.

If you want to be a millionaire and you currently have just $1,000 in the bank and earn $30,000 a year, chances are that it is going to take you some time to change from your current financial reality to millionaire status. Again, barring that lottery scenario – it won't happen fast.

If you are 30 pounds overweight, you can't lose 30 pounds overnight. You are going to have to do a variety of things differently than you are currently doing them (such as eating, drinking and exercising) and you are going to have to do them for a period of time – from 60 to 90 days or more. And once you reach your target weight, you are going to have to keep up with your new eating, drinking, and exercise habits if you want to maintain that weight.

The "truth" is that you cannot rush success. It takes hard work and commitment to both become and **remain** successful.

But this truth is not what most people want to hear. It seems that in our present culture, people try to rush success or at least the *illusion* of success all the time....

Think about the "credit craze" a few years ago. Fueled by access to easy credit, many people felt as though they could buy anything they wanted. So, many of them did. And they did so without any real thought as to how to pay for those things in the long term. Instead they bought things they felt they "deserved" to have and the result is that many of these people will be paying off those debts for years to come.

This is an example of rushing toward the *appearance* of financial success instead of first establishing those habits which can actually *create* financial success.

Consider people who use alcohol, drugs, or even food in order to change their mental state. Essentially, these people aren't happy with the way they feel, so they use various means as an escape. But this is a bad strategy for two reasons...

   i.   When the effects of the alcohol, drugs, or food wear off they still feel the same as they did before. And they can be even worse off, depending on the extent to which they over-indulged.

   ii.   Obviously the misuse of alcohol and other drugs causes long-term problems. But many things can be turned into a "drug," whether its food or some type of self-defeating behavior. And these behaviors simply add more layers to the underlying problem.

You can probably recall examples of how people try to rush or fake success. But it all boils down to one decidedly un-mysterious secret: there is only one way to get there. You must stay firmly rooted in reality and **do the work.**

Beware of Those Who Try to Hold You Back

As you start on the path of self-improvement and start making positive changes in your life, many people will encourage you, support you, and help you along the way. These people are invaluable and you should keep them close.

However, an unfortunate reality, a reality which comes as a shock to many, is that some people will become potential obstacles to your success. Worse still – the people who do this are sometimes those closest to you. And it is more common than you might think.

Imagine a woman who is overweight. She tells her best friend that she is going to start a healthy eating and exercise plan. Anyone who was truly supportive would encourage this woman because losing the weight, eating better and exercising would all be great things to do. Her health, self-image, and more would all logically improve as a result of this weight loss.

So why is it then that when her best friend (who is also overweight) hears about her idea, she says to her:

"You don't need to lose any weight; you look great the way you are."

The answer is simple. This particular friend feels threatened by her friend's potential future success. And instead of joining her friend on this weight loss journey, she finds it easier to withhold encouragement and resist this potential positive change. And although her "you look great" comment *sounds* positive, it is anything but. This is a type of stealth sabotage and is completely at odds with achieving success. You need to be able to recognize this sort of thing and move away from it as quickly as possible.

There are two types of negativity that manifest in others (including those people who are closest to you) when you attempt to make positive changes in your life. Especially when you embark on a journey towards achieving something exceptional...

i.   Covert Negativity

This kind of negativity can most easily be described as advice given to you "for your own good." Sometimes it can be sincere but misguided advice. Other times it can be because the person doesn't really want you to succeed because they feel threatened by your potential future success.

Here's an example that illustrates this point...

A couple of years ago, during a training class, I tore my right bicep tendon. In a split second, the muscle tore loose from the bone with a sickening popping sound. I immediately looked at my right arm and saw my bicep knotting up in a ball towards my right shoulder, leaving a large gap near the elbow. And just as suddenly, there was searing pain.

This injury was a potential game-changer for me, professionally speaking. In the short-term I was forced to cancel a large strength show which was just one week away. And in the longer term, I was unable to work on the security team for which I was the project manager. Because I had to learn to eat, shave and brush my teeth left-handed, I was in no position to carry weapons on a protection detail without the use of my right hand. Suddenly, there were just a lot of questions.

And it was while I waited for my surgery that it started. The advice. So much advice. All foisted upon me "for my own good." There were people who suggested that this injury was a sign that I should stop training "like a maniac." Others pointed out that bending horseshoes and steel bars must have somehow weakened my connective tissue. And the summations of their arguments were always that I should give up those "things I do." Particularly in light of the fact that I was about to turn 50. In short, this was all advice given to me for my own good.

The problem with advice that's "for your own good" is that it often comes at you during those times when you've been knocked down. And in my case, I was really having to stay focused in order to maintain my mental bearings. Because while I was awaiting surgery I was growing weaker, losing weight (nearly 20 pounds) and trying to figure out how I was ever going to take my useless right arm and train it back to the point that I could use it to roll up frying pans and shatter stacks of bricks.

Fortunately, I realized that this situation was tailor-made for applying the principles of **Mind Boss**…not because I was interested to see *if* they would work, but because at that time in my life I *had to* make them work.

In fact, just two days after the injury I made a list of things that I pledged to do until I had fully recovered from my injury. And the first one of those steps was just that: promising myself that I *would* recover. But beyond that, I needed a forward-looking goal. Something positive. Something **big**. And it was while lying on the sofa with my arm a sling, an arm that was now discolored black and purple, that I conceived of the stunt that I performed exactly one year and 13 days after my injury—a stunt that I envisioned as something worthy of Ripley's Believe it or Not.

The fact that this stunt (absorbing 6,000 pounds of impact force while lying on broken glass) was ultimately published and certified by Ripley's was truly gratifying and told me that I was on the right track with **Mind Boss**.

ii.   **Overt Negativity**

Overt negativity is of course easier to spot than covert negativity. Overt negativity can be distilled down to statements such as:

"You can't do that."

Many people allow such words to deter them and prevent them from taking action and achieving success. Do not fall into this trap. In this situation some tough love is required. Very often you will need to get yourself away from these people, no matter how close they are to you. You need to replace those negative voices with encouraging ones. You need to find people like my friend Jon Bruney.

People like Jon are the ones you want around if you want to be successful. Here's a story to highlight this point....

In my strongman shows I perform feats of strength. One of those feats is bending steel bars. As you might imagine, this *isn't* easy. Bar-bending was one of my favorite show feats to do and remained so until the day I saw an enormous strongman on a television show take TWO half-inch steel bars which had been duct-taped together and bend them completely in half. I was completely knocked out by this and immediately knew that someday, I wanted to be able to do the very same thing.

A couple of days later I had picked up some steel bars and brought them back to my garage. After wrapping them with duct-tape and with nobody around watching, I made my first attempt at bending those two bars. It was exhausting work, but I eventually got those bars bent in half. I was actually quite surprised when it happened. In fact, I was in such disbelief that several times that same day I went back to the garage to remeasure the diameter of the bars to verify for myself what I had done.

Several days later I was on the phone with Jon and I told him about the double-bar bend and how tough it was. And without missing a beat, he said to me, "That's cool, Mike, but I bet you could do three bars. Yeah, I definitely see you being able to do three someday." I then pointed out that three bars was insane, I had never seen it done, two bars had pretty much destroyed me, and a number of other reasons why three bars was impossible. But Jon's response was almost annoyingly consistent, "Mike, you are totally going to bend three bars someday."

So Jon had now planted a thought in my mind. It was a compelling thought, but it was an impossible-seeming thought. Nonetheless, I did eventually *try* three bars taped together. In fact I tried it two different times and it wasn't in the privacy of my garage. Both of those attempts were made during youth group presentations.

In both of these instances the attempted three-bar bend was not intended to be a "show stunt." Instead, I introduced the three bars to illustrate how, just like the young people seated before me, that even a "strongman" can come up against impossible-seeming challenges. And that many of life's challenges take place when it feels like the whole world is watching. I then told them that I had someone in my life who encouraged me to go past what I *knew* I could do (two bars) and to keep striving for something that *seemed* impossible for me to do (three bars).

And with that introduction, in full view of everyone present, I picked up three bars. Both times I pushed and pulled for what seemed like an eternity, (probably around two minutes). And both times the same thing happened: absolutely **nothing**. Those bars did not budge.

But the response to both of those two attempts amazed me. The rooms just erupted. It was a completely different response than I ever got from successfully slicing through a tall stack of bricks or bending a horseshoe. It may have been the integrity of the effort that people responded to. Those attempts had not been a matter of petty ego because they were too risky. Success was not only *not* guaranteed, it was highly unlikely—a fact which those audiences seemed to clearly understand.

The idea of bending three bars continued to stay with me. But I had basically resigned myself to the idea that the three-bar bend was going to stay in my life only as an object lesson. It was never going to be something that I'd actually ever be able to actually do. And I was okay with that. As I often say, "The things I do are not about *me*, they are about what I can inspire you to do."

Fast-forward to March of 2011 and I was presenting at an

event in Los Angeles. At the very end of this event, I told the group about my ongoing quest to bend three bars and that while it might remain impossible, at least for me, I was never going to stop trying.

And with that, I took three bars that were taped together and got ready for public attempt number three. And as I started, I immediately felt the same thing that I had felt the other two times: absolutely nothing. And soon I could feel that I was quickly running out of steam.

But then, something really strange happened, the bars started to bend, just a little. But that was all the motivation I needed. So I kept at it. And at it. It must have looked a bit unnerving for those who were watching. A slow, hard bend can be a bit uncomfortable to witness. But after approximately 4 minutes and 20 seconds (according to the video) I had pulled those three bars into a respectable U-shape.

So, a mere 15 months after Jon's initial suggestion – I had bent three steel bars, something that I had originally dismissed as "impossible." This is how powerful it is to surround yourself with the right people if you want to succeed.

What's the "moral" of this story?

Quite simply that the people you spend time with affect you. They influence you – both positively and negatively. If you want to be successful, choose the people you spend time with very carefully.

Here are some suggestions:

- If your goal is to become financially successful – spend time around people who have built wealth already. Some of whatever they did *will* rub off on you.

- If you want to lose weight, become fit and stay fit for the rest of your life – spend time with people who are already there. Their habits will impact you

- If you want to become good at something really specific – like black and white photography, landscape gardening, or boxing – spend time with people who are great at those things

- Whatever you want to become good at – spend time with people who are better than you in that area, because their "game" will bring yours up too. Always remember – you progress much faster if you have the courage to be the little fish in a big pond than if you insist on being the big fish in a small pond

- Cultivate integrity. Be prepared to give back to the people who help you. Relationships are a two-way street.

The theme of this chapter is to prepare you to prepare yourself. A prepared mind is a mind that can **focus** on goals with relentless intensity. The practice of focusing your mind is what we will work on now. Let's take a look at this chapter's exercise...

The FOCUSED Mind

To perform this exercise, seat yourself in a comfortable chair. Relax yourself physically and mentally. As you relax in your chair, find a point on the far wall. It can be any point—a spot of paint, a color on the wall, or anything you become aware of. Now begin to fix your attention on that spot. Don't remove your eyes from it. You will probably notice that you find yourself wanting to shift your gaze. Avoid doing so. If you find that you have briefly looked away, don't become defensive or feel defeated. Immediately return your attention to that same spot and continue.

Now take notice of how easy it is to direct your attention to a specific point that you have selected and to fully engage in this experience. Feel yourself being powerfully drawn to that point. Anytime an intrusive thought attempts to come to the forefront of your mind, allow yourself to brush away that thought in favor of your focus on that spot. Make yourself experience that spot. Notice its shape, color, texture, and any associations it might have for you. For just a few moments in time, let nothing exist other than that spot.

Now allow yourself to relax. Then acknowledge your efforts in performing this new exercise.

This may seem quite simple, but this is the nature of practice. Physical exercises are simple too, but no one questions their efficacy. By intentionally practicing the technique of directing your concentration to a specific spot, you can develop the skill of automatically directing your attention to those things in your life that require your attention.

This may be a conscious decision to focus on positive matters in order to better cope with a difficult situation. It can also be a circumstance where you must focus your attention onto a task that you find tedious or unpleasant, but still must be completed. The only way this exercise works is through practice. Through consistent effort, old habits of subconscious awareness or "default thinking" are replaced with intentionality. And intention is the essence of Mind Boss. It is the ability to direct your thoughts *when* and *where* you want them to go.

Three Suggestions

i.   Be careful not to confuse FEELINGS with REALITY. Always ask yourself: "Is the way I'm feeling a true reflection of the way things really are?"

   If the answer is "No" (which it often is), do the best you can to figure out the true nature of a situation and *then* take action. Remember – if you take action in the heat of the moment, based purely on the way you *feel* – you may do more harm than good.

ii. Surround yourself with positive people – people who will support you in all that you do and encourage you to achieve whatever you set your sights on.

Distance yourself (tactfully, if possible) from those people who may try to hold you back and whose attitudes and behavior get in the way of achieving your success. (Hopefully your eventual success will serve to inspire those same people.)

iii. In the next chapter we will be talking about PLANNING. To prepare yourself for that chapter, take a few minutes to establish where you are at right now in your life in a few key areas. In effect, this short exercise will allow you to become very clear about *your* current reality…

For the following areas, give yourself a score of 1 to 10. 10 would represent perfection with no room for improvement and 1 would be absolutely terrible. 5 is average.

Health / Physical Body – 4 / broken leg

Financial Situation – 6

Intimate Relationship – 7

Once you have given yourself a mark out of 10 for each of those three areas, write down the biggest success you're experiencing in each area as well as the biggest challenge.

For instance – for your health and physical body, you may score yourself a 7.

Your biggest success might be that you eat a very healthy diet 80% of the time.

Your biggest challenge might be that you're exercising only once a week.

Complete this exercise now, then proceed to Chapter 3...

1. A Health - Not able to exercise broken leg.

   B Eatng Healthy

2. A Gettng seat frtime on a wider range of equipment.

   B. I'm surrounded by people who are willing to train me.

3. A. Findng Time to be Intimate

   B. we get along very well, and have each other's back,

A = biggest successes

B = Biggest obstacl

CHAPTER 3: PLAN FOR SUCCESS

"If I had six hours to chop down a tree, I would spend the first
four hours sharpening the axe…."
Abraham Lincoln

Planning – The Third Tenet of Tough Thinking

The third part of our process is planning. Planning is how you
create a strategy to get you from where you are now to where you
want to be. Ideally, planning is the means by which you create a
blueprint for success.

Successful people plan well. They are master strategists. In
this chapter you will be introduced to principles that will enable you to become a master strategist too – someone who can
figure out how to make their goals a reality. You'll do this by
having an excellent plan. And an excellent plan starts with an
excellent goal.

How to Set Excellent Goals

Effective planning is comprised of the following components:

- A goal, or series of goals

- A series of steps and actions to achieve each goal

- Feedback mechanisms that allow you to assess your progress

It's not a long list. And the process is not nearly as complicated as some people might think. Despite that, people generally do not plan all that well. There are those who don't plan at all, so any results they experience are completely unpredictable. And there are those who do plan, but their plans are based on vague, nonspecific goals. Plans such as these are doomed to failure.

Here are three examples of some very common goals that illustrate what I'm talking about:

- "My goal is to lose weight."

- "My goal is to earn more money."

- "My goal is to find someone; I want to find the ONE."

Now this might initially seem a bit confusing. Because these goals *sound* good, don't they? After all, aren't those three goals common to so many people?

But it's not the target of these goals that is the problem. Instead it is the particular way that those goals are phrased. They are nonspecific.

This is a critical point, so here it is one more time... these goals are NONSPECIFIC. And an *absence* of specificity here will always lead to an *abundance* of disappointment.

These example goals don't really mean anything because they can't be defined. And without goal-specificity, you will not be able to chart a functional path to success.

So let's examine how to set *excellent* goals...

Excellent goals are realistic, specific, and challenging. Those three words – realistic, specific, and challenging – are key. A stated goal that lacks any one of these three key elements is a less-than-excellent goal.

The most successful people on the planet – whether wealthy entrepreneurs, top athletes, or accomplished academicians – are all examples of people who reap the rewards of realistic, specific and challenging goals.

Let's talk about the "realistic" part first....

When setting goals, you need to stay within the realms of possibility. Now this does ***not*** mean you should set boring, easily achievable goals that fail to inspire you.

But what is does mean is that if you are just over five feet tall, then setting your sights on playing NBA basketball is not a good goal because that sport is dominated by athletes who stand over six feet seven inches tall on average.

But here is a key point...I am not suggesting that you should give up basketball. You can still *love* basketball and still *play* basketball, but you have to understand that success in activities like sports requires not only talent and drive, but also requires having the right parents.

Nobody said that life was fair.

Here's another example. Have you ever watched an episode of one of those competitive singing shows on television and seen tearful contestants arguing with the panel of judges? These would-be vocalists protest the judge's verdict and say things like "But music is my life" or "This is all I've ever wanted to do."

Now if you're anything like me, after listening to some of their unfortunate vocal interpretations, you're wondering how in the world these people could *not know* that they can't sing. Being a professional singer is another case where drive and determination are great, but if you haven't been blessed with a voice that people want to listen to, you are not going to be a star.

Hey, if you love to sing, that's great. Sing all you like. But you need to be honest enough with yourself to determine whether you have something that the rest of the world wants to hear.

So once you're ready to be "real" with yourself, ask the question "Do I have what it takes to become excellent at this?" Now this is a different question from "Is what I want to do difficult?" Difficult we can handle. Difficult means you're thinking in the right direction. Difficult and even unreasonable goals are fantastic. I love goals like that and you can learn to love them too. But, the first part of an excellent goal is that it is REALISTIC.

The second part of an excellent goal is that it is SPECIFIC.

Think back to these three examples of nonspecific goals...

  – "My goal is to lose weight."

  – "My goal is to earn more money."

  – "My goal is to find someone; I want to find the ONE."

Not one of these goals is specific. And as I pointed out previously, without specificity a satisfactory level of success will not be achieved.

Let's take a closer look at this first goal...

  – "My goal is to lose weight."

If someone were to approach me with that goal, I'd say – "Okay, fine – but before we proceed any further, we need to figure some things out." And then I'd ask some questions:

"*Exactly* how much weight would you like to lose…10 pounds? 25 pounds? Some other (specific) amount?"

"By what date would you like to lose this weight… meaning WHEN would you like to lose it by?"

So now let's say that you've told me you'd like to lose 20 pounds in the next 4 months.

There it is.

We now have a specific, measurable goal. You have said *exactly* how much weight you would like to lose (20 pounds) and you have said *when* you would like to lose it by (in the next 4 months). You have an exact number and a precise date.

And that's the difference?

Original goal (vague):

"My goal is to lose weight."

New goal (specific and measurable):

"I want to lose 20 pounds in the next 4 months."

And by the way – that goal is not only specific, it's also realistic.

The third part of setting excellent goals is to make your goals CHALLENGING.

When a goal is challenging, it provides the inspiration and motivation necessary to take the action required to make that goal come to life.

Consider the following three goals:

- A marathon runner who has a personal best of 2 hours and 55 minutes who wants to shave 12 minutes off his time over the next 10 years.

- A young lawyer working in New York City wants to go from his current entry-level position at the firm he works for to being a partner within the next 12 years.

- A 40-year-old woman wants to lose 35 pounds of body weight in the next 6 months.

Two of those goals are challenging and one is not. Can you spot which one of the goals is *not*?

I'll help you out... It's the first one.

Aspiring to shave a mere 12 minutes off a marathon time over the next 10 years is hardly inspirational. This is an example of a goal that is both realistic and specific (which is good), but is just far too *easy*. And one thing is for certain – easy goals are not the path to a high level of achievement and fulfilment.

In contrast to the marathon runner's non-challenging (and therefore non-excellent) original goal, the other two examples are challenging...

Becoming a partner in a New York law firm is a challenging prop-
osition, but it's still within the realm of possibility because of the
12 year time-frame.

Likewise, losing 35 pounds in 6 months is challenging – it will
require sustained, disciplined effort – but it's entirely realistic at
the same time.

Both of these goals are specific because they have definite outcomes and a precise time frame.

Realistic, specific, and challenging goals are crucial for your success. Such goals help you decide WHAT you want and WHEN
you want it.

But there is a third component to the planning phase.

The third component is the "HOW."

Exactly *how* are you going to get *what* you want, *when* you want it?

This is when you need to....

Have a Plan

Although most people don't do it, setting goals that are realistic,
specific and challenging is actually the *easy* part.

Think about it...

How difficult is it to get out a piece of paper or open up your computer and write down WHAT you want and WHEN you would like to have it by?

Not very difficult at all. In fact, I'm willing to bet that you could take out a piece of paper right now and in a matter of minutes write down a dozen or so realistic, specific, challenging goals that would both look and sound great.

The more difficult part comes when you ask yourself this question:

"Okay, I now know *what* I want and *when* I want to achieve it by, but **how** exactly am I going to make it happen?"

This is where you have to come up with a PLAN. Your plan is the roadmap you will use to bring those goals to life.

And if you want your plan to be effective, your plan will need a "strategic philosophy." The strategic philosophy of **Mind Boss** is this:

—   The best strategy is the one that gets you to your goal *as fast as possible* and *with the least amount of effort*

This philosophy may sound as though it discounts the value of hard work. But it doesn't. We always presume hard work. Hard work is inherent to any successful undertaking. The point is that to use more time and effort than is necessary to get the job done is not working *smart*. And the whole point of **Mind Boss** is to apply maximum effort toward amazing goals as intelligently as possible.

So what you want is an *efficient* plan, and efficiency means…getting maximum results in the quickest time possible, and with the least amount of effort expended in the process.

Elite athletes understand this only too well. For instance, if you could win an Olympic medal in any event you liked, would you rather train three hours a day to get there or ten?

It's a no-brainer. You would do it in three hours a day if possible. The ten-hour plan is not efficient (assuming both plans brought about the same outcome – an Olympic medal in your chosen event).

One thing to keep in mind is that very often the most efficient plan is the SIMPLEST one. Complexity for the sake of complexity is a waste of time.

Consider a simple weight-loss scenario….

Jenny is 40 years old and weighs 165 pounds. Her goal is to lose 35 pounds over the next 20 weeks and end up at 130 pounds – the weight she used to be when she was 25 and healthy. This would mean that she needs to lose an average of 2 pounds a week. This is entirely doable…it's a realistic, specific, and challenging goal.

Let's take a look at a simple, efficient plan that she could use to get down to her goal weight of 130 pounds.

The plan is divided into two clear areas:

   –   Nutrition (what Jenny eats and drinks)

and...

   –   Exercise

Let's deal with nutrition first...

Jenny's current diet is full of problem areas. She drinks a lot of soda and eats mostly fast food. The majority of her food choices are processed and full of sugar, which is not good for her waistline or her health.

Here is her simple 8-step nutritional plan for the next 20 weeks:

1. Eliminate soda and drink at least 2 liters of water a day

2. Coffee is limited to 2 cups per day

3. Alcohol is limited to 3 glasses of wine per week

4. Fast food is off the menu and will be replaced with home-cooked, unprocessed, natural food choices that emphasize lean protein sources and vegetables

    She may eat out twice a week while on her plan, but she will stick to the same types of foods referenced in point #4

5. Will eat 3 meals a day – breakfast, lunch, and dinner

6. Will not snack between meals

7.   Will only eat until satiated – not until stuffed

And here is Jenny's exercise plan for the next 20 weeks…

Keep in mind that Jenny had been exercising 1 to 3 times a week before starting her diet, but had no set routine or plan.

–   Exercise 3 times a week following a prescribed program. The emphasis of these sessions will be on resistance training

–   Will walk the other 4 days a week. These walks will last between 20 and 60 minutes

As you can see, both Jenny's nutritional plan and exercise plan are fairly simple. But simplicity should not be confused with a lack of effectiveness.

The aim of the nutritional plan is to minimize the amount of empty calories Jenny is eating. The aim of the fitness plan is to get Jenny training every day and to do so with a mix of resistance and aerobic exercise.

If Jenny follows the eight steps in her nutritional plan and the two steps in her exercise plan, she will achieve those objectives and lose weight. Now, will she lose *exactly* 35 pounds in 20 weeks?

We can't say for certain. And, not to sound too cavalier here, but who cares?

The important thing is that the plan is sufficient to get her off to an excellent start. And once begun, it is a simple matter to adjust the plan along the way if necessary (but more on that later).

For now, just remember that you don't need the "perfect plan" to get started. You just need a good plan. And once you have a good plan, it's time to take action. As soon as you do that, you will get results. And those results should serve to motivate and inspire you to *keep* taking action and move closer and closer towards the realization of your goal.

But, before you put your plan into action, you need the final piece of the puzzle. You need to...

Install "Feedback Mechanisms"

Every plan needs a feedback mechanism to let you know whether the plan is working effectively or not.

It doesn't make sense to draw up a plan and then stick to it dogmatically even if it's failing. Yet people do this. Often it is because their plan was so poorly developed in the first place that they don't realize it's failing.

Your feedback mechanisms do not need to be complicated to be effective. You just need to remember to install them into your plans.

Let's take a look at a few examples of good and not-so-good feedback mechanisms. We'll carry on with the previous scenario concerning Jenny's fat loss goal. Here are the feedback mechanisms she will use.

Every Monday during the course of her 20-week regimen she is going to do the following things, immediately after she gets out of bed at 7:30 a.m:

—   Weigh herself

—   Measure her waist, hips, and thighs

Do you think that those two data points (body weight and site-measurements) would be good feedback mechanisms to determine whether her exercise and meal plan is proving successful or not?

If you said "yes," you would be right. Weight and measurements are easy to track and numbers are objective.

Those two simple steps will quickly and clearly indicate whether Jenny's plan is working or not. Weighing herself will enable her to see how close she is to her ongoing goal of losing two pounds a week. And the site measurements indicate specifically where she is losing the weight and will serve to provide the motivation to keep going.

So in this instance we have feedback mechanisms which are very simple and very effective.

Contrast this with another feedback mechanism example:

—   Weighing yourself two times per day

—   Measuring the waist, hips, and thighs once every day

Now rather than providing quality feedback about the success of a diet plan, this example would best be described as data collection run amok. The frequency of these measurements would drive most people crazy. It's too much measuring being done on a far too frequent basis.

First, there is no productive point in weighing oneself two times a day. A person's weight will not fluctuate enough to necessitate this level of scrutiny. And the same goes for the measurements. From one day to the next, these measurements will not vary in a meaningful way. And to over-obsess about collecting this kind of information is both a waste of time and an exercise in frustration.

There is a clear difference with these two approaches.

To take things to the other extreme, a poorly applied feedback mechanism would be to take these same body-weight and site measurements on a monthly basis. The problem with this example is that the measurements are being taken far too infrequently. Such an approach would allow a failing plan to continue for several weeks undetected.

This next point is important...

The quality of the feedback mechanisms you use can determine whether your plan will succeed or fail.

The reason for this is that if you choose poorly (as illustrated with the examples I just listed), you are likely to wind up so frustrated that you will give up, no matter how good your plan looks. In other words – the wrong feedback mechanism can make a good plan appear as though it is failing.

A good feedback mechanism *should* show you the way things really are. It should show you the **reality** of the situation – not better, not worse. And that is valuable feedback. Skewed or distorted feedback that makes a bad situation *appear* great when it is not, or vice versa, is of no use.

Let's take look at a couple of other examples of feedback collection....

Imagine a young man who is training to become a world-class sprinter. He has been spotted by a sprint coach and it is obvious to the coach that this athlete has the *potential* to become extremely fast. In fact, this athlete appears to be capable of eventually running 100 meters in less than ten seconds – a potential world-class performer.

But presently, our young sprinter's personal best is 10.98 seconds at 18 years of age – still a ways off of a sub-10 second 100 meter time.

So how will the coach measure the success of his pupil's training program?

Well, he *could* use a feedback mechanism that looks for a sub-10-second 100-meter time each time the athlete competes. But this would be a non-productive feedback mechanism because it would most likely lead the athlete to feel poorly about his capabilities.

Here's why…

Despite the super-fast nature of the event, a sprinter cannot go from 10.98 to sub-10 seconds overnight. Shaving off almost an entire second in the 100 meters requires incremental improvements over time. And over time those speed improvements might look more like this:

10.90

10.85

10.81

10.76

10.75

10.60

And so on….

These decreases in time (speed improvements) will not always come in predictable increments (as shown in the above example) and our sprinter may have meets where either his times do not improve or he runs an even slower race.

Because of the imprecise nature of sprinting performance from race to race, the coach might use a feedback mechanism that tracks how frequently our sprinter was setting personal bests. For example, if the sprinter was consistently setting personal bests every 16 weeks – then both athlete and coach should consider their training program a success.

Once you have your feedback mechanisms in place, you are ready to put your plan into action and get to work. As you do this, it's important to...

Be Flexible

The purpose of feedback mechanisms is to show you whether or not your plan is working as well as you would like it too.

If your plan *is* working – that's great – you just carry on.

But what if your feedback mechanisms show you that your plan is *not* working or that certain parts of your plan are not working as effectively as they could be doing?

This is where you need to be flexible.

To be successful, you will need to be prepared to make changes as necessary. There might even be a point where you opt to scrap a plan entirely and start over from scratch.

An agile, flexible mindset is an attribute common to successful people. Remember – your plan is simply a means to an end – the "end state" being your GOAL. So avoid becoming too emotionally attached to a plan, especially if it is not getting the job done.

If you do decide to make changes in your plan, it is important to only adjust one thing at a time if possible. When you modify one thing at a time it is easy to see whether or not this change has a positive effect. On the contrary, if you adjust many things at once, it becomes almost impossible to tell exactly which of those changes brought about positive change and which ones didn't help at all.

So, before making an adjustment to your plan – based on what your feedback mechanism has told you – ask yourself this question:

"What is the one thing that I can change in my plan which will yield the biggest possible positive effect on my results?"

Answer that question carefully and then make your change. Then get back to business. Work hard and track your progress to see if you were correct. If not, make another adjustment. With enough persistence and an analytic approach, you will eventually arrive at the plan that gets you to your goal.

Another thing to consider is that you need to be flexible with regard to your goals. Sometimes making changes to a **goal** is necessary. In fact, this is more common than you might think.

Here are some examples:

- Losing 50 pounds in 16 weeks

- Earning an MBA in two years while working full-time

- Earning a black belt in karate within the next 3 years

All of those are great goals. They are specific and measurable. (And yes, that is yet *another* weight-loss example. Because weight-loss is the undisputed "number one" self-improvement topic, I reference it frequently.)

But here's the thing...

As somebody sets out on their journey to try to accomplish any one of those goals, it may become apparent midway into the process that the goal itself needs to change – either because it was a little too ambitious, or not ambitious enough.

For instance...

- Maybe the 50-pound fat loss goal will actually require 22 weeks instead of 16 weeks

- Perhaps the adult student will need to add another semester to their plan to ensure that they maintain the grade-point average goal they had set. (A smaller goal within a larger goal.)

- And the promising karate student can actually earn his black belt within the next 2.5 years instead of 3.

In those examples the **time frame** of the goals changed.

Sometimes the **outcome** can be modified too...

- The person wanting to lose 50 pounds may realize that in fact they need to lose only 40 pounds.

- The adult student might find that their advanced degree program provides an opportunity to spend a semester abroad to study business in an international setting.

- The karate student may decide to train beyond his first black belt and continue to pursue a higher level of mastery during those 3 years.

Plans and goals should both be flexible. And you should likewise be flexible in the execution of your plan and the attainment of your goals. Flexibility in this case does not imply a lack of strength on your part. No one questions the strength of a skyscraper. But while they must be strong to serve their purpose, they must also flex in response to environmental conditions. It is the steel in a skyscraper's frame that enables it to be strong yet flexible. When it comes to accomplishing your goals, you too need to be strong and flexible. You need to be like steel.

It is my hope that once you start down the road of deliberate goal attainment, you find it to be a positive addiction. Your initial successes should beget future successes. Appreciate your current accomplishments but always with an eye towards future goals. This way of thinking keeps you creative, ambitious and motivated. If you want superior results in life, you must think like a chess player – always a few moves ahead.

Exercise

This exercise will allow you to practice the process of goal-setting for yourself. Ideally you will come up with some inspiring goals that you feel compelled to make happen. Inspirational goals are the kind that get you up early in the morning and keep you up till late because they're both exciting and meaningful.

There are two parts to this exercise:

i.   Setting long-term goals
ii. Creating a plan for the next 90 days

The idea of this exercise is that you state your long-term goals and then you come up with a plan of action for the next 90 days. The 90-day plan will get you started and well on your way toward making your long-term goals a reality.

Divide your long-term goals into five key areas:

–   Physical Goals

- Financial Goals

- Relationship Goals

- Enjoyment / Adventure Goals

- Contribution / Service Goals

Physical goals relate to everything to do with your physical body. Goals that have to do with health, longevity, and so on would go in this section. This would also be the place for any athletic or sports performance goals.

Financial goals relate to everything to do with your job, career, business, investments, and so on. Specific goals regarding debt reduction/elimination and wealth accumulation would also fit into this section.

Relationship goals relate to everything to do with how you interact with people. Intimate relationships, family relationships, work relationships, and any goals to do with friends would fit into this section.

Enjoyment and adventure goals are those things you dream of acquiring and adventures you want to experience. Perhaps you would like to own a sports car, learn to play a musical instrument, buy a vacation home or visit the Seven Wonders of the World. Whatever the case – write it down.

Contribution and service goals are where you set goals that have to do with helping other people. It's not a common practice to set contribution goals, but it's an amazing thing to do. So start seeing yourself as someone who can help make the world a better place and come up with some goals for this section.

And before we leave the topic of service, let's dispel a common misconception about helping others. You don't have to be a wealthy philanthropist or someone with all kinds of time on their hands in order to make a difference in the world. Even when my family was living on cop's salary we made a concerted effort to give where we could. One of these ways that didn't require a large investment was to sponsor needy children in other parts of the world. Lots of people do this, but the way that we approached it was to have each one of our children be in charge of a different sponsored child. So from youngest to oldest, each Gillette kid had a kid "of their own." They all took an active role in sharing information about *their* kid through the letters and updates we would receive from places like Guatemala, India, and the Philippines. It was always a special occasion when we would get an updated photograph of those children, which we would put up on the refrigerator (a place of significance in the Gillette house) alongside our other family photographs.

There are, of course, numerous ways to serve others. Once you start looking within your own community you'll likely find a variety of ways to impact your corner of the world. And if you're already an active "helper" in the world, take a little time to specifically plan your "help." You'll discover that by being more strategic in the way that you approach service, there will be even more of you to go around.

As you write down your goals, you may discover a goal that doesn't seem to fit into any one of the five categories above, and that's okay. If that happens, write the goal down anyway – fitting your goals into the categories is not the most important thing. The important thing is to identify your goals and then devise a plan to make them happen.

Let's get started with the exercise...

Begin this exercise by writing down long-term goals for each of the five sections:

- Physical Goals

- Financial Goals

- Relationship Goals

- Enjoyment & Adventure Goals

- Contribution & Service Goals

It should be fairly easy to come up with a goal for each one of these categories so let me challenge you to come up several for each section.

When you write down your long-term goals, think of "long-term" in the context of a significant accomplishment. It does not have to be 5 or 10 years away. Also keep in mind that these long-term goals can vary in length.

For instance, in the physical goals section you might indicate that you want to lower your blood pressure by 30 points. That's a good long-term goal, and yet in actuality it may only take 8 to 10 months.

In contrast, in your financial goals section you may record that you want to become a lawyer. To do this you know you will need to attend law school and then pass the Bar Exam. So depending on whether you will be a full- or part-time student, this long-term goal might be more like a 3- to a 5- year goal.

In this context we are not using long-term to denote a set amount of years. Instead, long-term simply means "things that are important to you." Consider long-term goals to be accomplishment milestones.

So begin now and come up with your long-term goals for each of these five sections:

- Physical Goals

- Financial Goals

- Relationship Goals

- Enjoyment / Adventure Goals

– Contribution / Service Goals

You can prioritize the goals later. And don't worry about going into great amounts of detail when writing down your long-term goals. Just lay out what you want to achieve in a sentence or two for each one.

Once you have recorded your long-term goals, you can then create your 90-day plan for each one.

In contrast with the long-term goal-setting portion of this exercise, where all you did was write down a sentence or two for each goal, your 90-day plan will require a higher level of detail.

Here are some examples to illustrate what I mean...

Let's say that in your physical goals section you have decided that you'd like to run your first half-marathon (13 miles) within the next year. But at the present time you haven't done any serious training.

Here's how your 90-day plan might look:

In the next 7 days you would...

– Buy a quality pair of running shoes

– Buy some suitable clothes for wear while running

– Join a running club (so that you are surrounded by like-minded individuals who you can train with and learn from)

–   Commit to training 5 days a week

–   Start training!

Those are fairly obvious things that need to be done as soon as possible, hence the 7 day time frame.

In your 90-day plan you also state that you will…

–   Get at least 8 hours of sleep a night and plan to go to bed at the same time every day

–   Develop a sound nutrition plan

–   Lose 12 pounds

The nutrition plan will need to be monitored because at present you aren't sure exactly how much food you will need to eat given the amount of training you are going to be doing.

So this is one of those situations where you have to come up with a plan – in this case a nutrition plan – put it into action, and use your feedback mechanisms to tell you if the plan is working or whether it needs to be changed.

You may decide you want to lose 1.5 pounds a week – so that's your feedback mechanism. If you lose 1.5 pounds a week, you stick with the plan. If you gain weight, you eat a little less. If you lose weight too fast, you eat a little more.

Once you have your 90-day plan, you will want to "Red-Team" it.

Red-Teaming is a concept that comes from the military. It is the practice of deliberately trying to find weaknesses or vulnerabilities, most often those associated within a military facility. These vulnerabilities can be physical, such as a security fence or a perimeter alarm. But they can also be human-related. In these cases, specially assigned personnel (referred to as Red-Teams) will attempt to get past security guards, either by surreptitious means or an overt ruse.

So Red-Team your plan. Probe it for weaknesses, vague language, and non-specific outcomes. When you are finally ready to "go to battle" to hunt down your goals, you'll be more confident with a plan that's been tested.

Now don't get stuck on the numerical aspect of 90 days. This is not a set-in-stone number. Its purpose in the short term is to get you to TAKE ACTION. Because it is only when you take action and apply sustained effort that you begin to get results and move towards making your long-term goals a reality.

Let's consider a totally different long-term goal...

Let's imagine that you had written down that you would like to purchase a $500,000 home in four years' time.

In this example you also want to purchase the home with a $100,000 down payment. And you also expect to make a $20,000 profit when you sell your existing home. This leaves you with

$80,000 to find, or $20,000 per year for the next four years.

This works out to: $1666.67 per month

Your 90-day plan may look like this:

— Open a new savings account, with the highest rate of interest possible, specifically for the deposit for your new house

— Each month, when you get paid, you will immediately go online and transfer $1700.00 into your savings account (you decide to round $1666.67 up to $1700.00 in order to give you a slightly higher deposit)

— Examine your current expenses and try to save $200.00 a month. You need to do this because you currently can comfortably afford to save $1500.00 from your income, but not $1700.00.

As you can see, this 90-day plan is fairly straightforward. And it could very well work for the next four years, all the way up to the point where you had saved $80,000 and were ready to buy your house.

Here's how this exercise looks in summary

— Write down your long-term goal

— Develop your 90-day plan

– Red-Team your plan

– Put your plan into action

– Use feedback mechanisms to tell you how well your plan is working and if any changes need to be made

– Adjust your plan where necessary to maximize results

You can use these six simple steps whenever you come up with a long-term goal.

Three Suggestions

i. Use the exercise in this chapter to identify your long-term goals and then come up with 90-day action plans for each goal

ii. Keep in mind that goals and plans can change and the ability to know when things need to change is one of the prerequisites for success. Always make sure your plans have clear feedback mechanisms that show you how effectively your plans are working. These feedback mechanisms should tell you when something needs changing without any guesswork on your part. Guessing is the antithesis of a well-thought out strategy. Above all, keep an open mind and be flexible in your approach – otherwise you won't be able to act upon the information that your feedback mechanisms provide

Never leave a goal-setting and planning exercise without doing something towards making your goal happen. Taking IMMEDI-ATE action is one of the hallmarks of a winner. Procrastination on the other hand, is not. It is a defining characteristic of people who never fully realize their dreams.

CHAPTER 4: PERFECTING PERSISTENCE

"Nothing in this world can take the place of persistence. Talent will not; nothing is more common than unsuccessful people with talent. Genius will not; unrewarded genius is almost a proverb. Education will not; the world is full of educated derelicts. Persistence and determination alone are omnipotent..."

– Calvin Coolidge

Persistence – The Fourth Tenet of Tough Thinking

There are those people who successfully overcome their fear. They find the purpose that allows them to blast through the fear that stands in the way of just getting started. And once started, they keep going. They stare reality in the face, harboring no false illusions about what it takes to press forward toward their goals. They plan well and they pursue their plan. And yet, after all that work has been accomplished, they will still FAIL.

How can this be?

Because they have not perfected the art of PERSISTENCE.

Persistence. Discipline. **Toughness.** Whatever you choose to call it, it is the most essential part of the equation. And if it is in short supply, you will run out of it.

When things are going well, it's easy to carry on, to stay positive and press forward. But what happens when the going gets tough? What happens when things don't go according to your plan? What will you do then?

Will you give up, or will you have enough persistence to carry you through?

Sadly, many people do give up. They surrender. And these can be intelligent, competent people. Their problem is not a lack of talent or skill. Rather, they lack *capacity*. They, for whatever reason, don't have (or don't *think* they have) the capacity to endure for the long haul.

The business section of your local bookstore (assuming you still have a local bookstore) is full of accounts of very successful people who have experienced failure. In many cases they failed multiple times. But instead of seeing their failed ventures as the end of their journey and giving up – they saw them as learning opportunities – and their persistence carried them forward. Forward to success.

In contrast, there are those people, (perhaps you even know of some), who have quit their jobs and started a business, only to see that business fail. And that's it – they abandoned their dreams, returned to a 9-to-5 job, and their dreams were eventually forgotten.

What's the difference? Persistence.

Persistence – that ability to tough things out and carry on, even when things become difficult – is a common attribute of successful people. Success is deeply rooted in toughness.

And although persistence is an invaluable commodity, it is frequently misunderstood. There are those who mistake persistence for adhering blindly to what might be a failing course of action, or remaining willfully oblivious to situational variables.

But persistence is none of those things. This is why we spent so much time discussing the importance of feedback mechanisms and having a good plan in the first place. Because being persistent should never be synonymous with being stupid. It is more accurate to describe persistence as a powerful patience. When you are patient, you do not fret about things. You are unshakeable.

And this goes back to the importance of creating goals that you are truly passionate about. It is far easier to think tough when your goals are inspirational. Anything less than that makes it easy to turn your back when the road turns rough. If your goals are inspirational enough, persistence, to a large degree, can take care of itself.

But since your goals are too important to leave anything to

chance, we will spend some more time learning about toughness. We will explore what it means to be tough and how to demonstrate toughness "on-demand."

This is the art of persistence...

The Persistent Mindset

With a persistent mindset, you enhance your ability to deal with stressors– physical, mental, and emotional – the very things that grind people down and cause them to quit.

Mindset is not something static and it is not innate. Mental fortitude is as trainable as any other skill. It typically seems a bit mysterious, but this is because most people either don't think much about it, or take the time to study this realm of personal development.

The chief reason for training your mindset is that through the persistent application of thinking tough, you can supersede the kinds of results that are reliant upon talent alone. Listen, it is great to possess intellect and skill. But it is the *persistent application* of your intellect and skill that allows you to discover your real limits and achieve your true potential.

Some years back I had had the good fortune to visit with wrestling legend Dan Gable. Gable is a true legend who completely dominated his chosen sport as both an athlete and coach. In the days when Gable was competing as an athlete, it was not his technical skill that made him so formidable, it was his indomitable mental toughness, a singular toughness exemplified in this quote:

"My obvious goals were there; State Champion, NCAA Champion and Olympic Champion. To get there I set an everyday goal which was to push myself to exhaustion or, in other words, to work so hard in practice that someone would have to carry me off the mat...."

That's a lot of wisdom in just one quote. Here is Dan Gable, one of the most accomplished athletes of the 20th century, in a mere two sentences, attesting to the importance of setting long-term achievement goals, short-term training goals, and manifesting relentless persistence. His words suggest that we are on the right track.

Here's another illustration of mental toughness from the world of sports, Tiger Woods.

From 1997 until late 2009, Woods was the dominant force in professional golf. This dominance was facilitated by a lethal combination of technical skill and mental and physical strength. Beyond his mastery of the root skills of golf, Woods was unique in the way he had embraced weight-training. He was the first notable golfer to use strength-training as a means to craft the ideal golfer's physique. He also had been introduced to the mental training techniques of hypnosis and sports psychology going all the way back to the age of 13. In a sport where a player's mindset is a make-or-break commodity, during this 12-year period, Woods seemed unstoppable.

Now there is an old expression about the internal nature of golf which states that "Golf is 90% mental..." And while that percentage might be inexact, few would debate the critical role that the mind serves in the outcome of a successful round of play. And there has been no clearer example of how a distracted, uncontrolled mind renders a professional golfer helpless than the formerly unstoppable Woods.

When the private affairs of Tiger Woods became public, the sports world witnessed the unravelling of a superman. The scrutiny and pressures were unrelenting and the result was an alarmingly abrupt change in the state of Woods' performance.

The reason that this example is so important to study is that Woods had begun a quantifiable freefall down the rankings. His legendarily tough mindset had been damaged in the wake of his scandals and his tournament play was likewise affected.

Now (and this is the critical part) Woods had not lost any of his technical skill. He was still a stronger athlete than almost all of his competitors. So physically speaking, we could say he was the same golfer that he was before. But what Woods had lost was on the *inside*. The veneer of mental toughness that had kept him so far ahead of his contemporaries for so long had finally been cracked.

Woods had strayed from the plan that had served him so well for so long. The feedback mechanism of that old plan was now clearly showing that his new "plan" was not working. And the reality of that new plan was Woods had been leading a logistically and geographically complex double life.

An armchair psychologist might even conclude that Woods had become disconnected from his original purpose for golf– purpose that had become secondary to the spoils of a gratification-driven, celebrity lifestyle.

Diligent Doses of Discipline

The persistent mindset is the path to discipline. Or, what some people refer to as "self-discipline." Discipline is an interesting attribute. Most people would say that they would like to have more of it, but they tend to regard it as something unpleasant. To put it another way, people often think of discipline like a kind of food that that while "good for you," just tastes bad.

So what *is* discipline exactly? It is the quality that can enable an athlete to train relentlessly, without benefit of a formalized support structure like a coach, team, or training partner. In another context, someone who consistently makes the "right" choices for themselves in life could be said to possess *self*-discipline.

When I was in the military, the term discipline was often used in association with doing things that you did not really want to do. These were generally things that caused fatigue, pain, fear, or all of the above. And even though the term discipline is frequently attached to unpleasant or tedious tasks, most people still say that they wished they had more discipline in their lives.

Consider this: in the late 1990s I ran a commercial martial arts school. I taught Jiu-Jitsu to children between the ages of 6 through 18 years. And during the entire time I operated that school, I never had a single parent bring in their child specifically because they wanted their child to learn Jiu-Jitsu. Not once. What these parents *did* tell me is that they wanted their child to develop *discipline.*

And discipline is of course not just for kids. Here's another example. My very first athlete clients were all women and they were all fighters…fighters as in kickboxers and grapplers. And like their male counterparts, they competed in specific weight divisions. The big challenge for these athletes is to stay strong and healthy while maintaining, or, if necessary, losing weight.

So in the course of those activities I would get asked the question: "Mike, what should I be eating?" Now these are smart, experienced women, so I would answer like this: "You already *know* what things to eat, just eat those things."

But this was where the paradox would appear, in their responses. And how would they respond? Like this: "Mike, I *know* that I know what to eat, I just want *you* to **tell me** to eat those things."

So even among these very tough, *seemingly* disciplined athletes there was a missing ingredient—a lack of self-discipline or mental toughness. And like the athletes in this example, we all generally know what we should do. We know that we need to work hard to accomplish things of significance. But even when we know this, it can still be a hard thing to do.

This takes us right back to the idea that persistent discipline equates to persistent toughness. So we all probably agree that we want to have "it"…but where does "it" come from? Here's what some "experts" have said about this topic.

In a recent study published in the Journal of Applied Sport Psychology, a group of international-level athletes in a variety of sports were asked to develop a definition of mental toughness. They concluded that, within the diverse demands of competitive sport, mental toughness involves having a "psychological edge" that enables one to cope better than one's opponents. Furthermore, mental toughness involves a consistent ability to remain determined, focused, confident, and in control under pressure.

Perhaps the moral of this story may be that super-talented people, such as the athletes who were interviewed, aren't always the best at explaining why they are successful. But this makes sense, as it is an athlete's job to execute, whereas it is a coach's job to plan. So in this case, we might have learned more by hearing from the coaches. And in *your* case (unless you work with someone like me), you are both the athlete *and* the coach, so you are in charge of planning *and* execution).

The results of this study don't actually take us any further in terms of understanding the topic. The conclusions were really just a summary of descriptions of the characteristics of mental toughness.

The "mystery" of discipline might be better understood if we go back to considering what it looks like in action rather than by examining it as it sits upon a metaphorical shelf. Back in the early 1990s, my kids frequently listened to a song by the group DC Talk called "Love is a Verb." And the simple clarity of that title hit me hard. It is the age-old idea that actions speak louder than words, distilled down to a rather simple-sounding song title. Deep.

And just like love, discipline is best understood in its active state. Therefore discipline is not our purpose and it is not our preparations, or even our plan. Discipline is the manifestation of our persistence. It is when we persist, when we hang on and do the work. *That* is discipline. Discipline is found in **doing**.

Here is one of my favorite examples of this idea, illustrated in a quote which has often been attributed to self-disciplinarian extraordinaire Bruce Lee, but actually originated from 19th Century German writer Johann Goethe: "Knowing is not enough; we must *apply*. Willing is not enough; we must *do*...."

That's it right there. Discipline. Completely contained within this very tough yet very elegant statement. This quote also illuminates the paradox that just because something is simple to describe, it does not mean that it is necessarily easy to have. And so it goes with discipline. Life is choices. And strong choices, those choices that can take you the furthest, can be the hardest ones to execute.

Of course once we start throwing around names like Bruce Lee, attitudes about discipline and toughness start to coalesce over on the physical side of the spectrum. But discipline is not just the province of the physically inclined. It is, rather, a universal quality that is manifested by any high achiever, from the triathlete to the musician to the stay-at-home mom who is also a full-time college student. Discipline is the common denominator of intentional destiny.

In my years working as a bodyguard, I learned quite a bit about the art of persistence. I was able to see it up close as I watched clients engage in daily doses of discipline. The company I worked for primarily served "regulars" as opposed to casual or one-time clients. These regulars were, for the most part, high net-worth types from the technology industry. And they were all stunningly smart. There was much to learn by spending time around them, and I am smart enough to pay attention to what smart people do.

All of those clients were about as successful as any person could be. They all worked hard and were all very passionate about what they did. But in addition to that, they also possessed tremendous self-discipline. The amount of work they could pack into a day was extraordinary.

Part of this efficiency of effort came from well-honed routines. There was nothing random about the way they operated. There was a reason or purpose to how they spent their time and in the precise order that they did things. And this *conscious consistency* allowed them to not only get a lot of work done, but also appeared to reduce the stress and anxiety that many people feel as result of their own less-than-organized lifestyles.

To cultivate this same kind of efficiency in your life, here are a few suggestions to get you started. And remember, many things only *seem* difficult until you try them. If you make a real effort, you'll usually find that they're no big deal. So give these a go and see if *your* efficiency doesn't improve:

- Go to bed at the same time every night and wake up at the same time each day. Seriously, just try it.

- Develop a "morning ritual" that gets you ready for the day. This should take up the first 30-60 minutes of your day and could consist of a 20-minute walk, a refreshing shower, 10 minutes of meditation, and a healthy break-fast. The activities are up to you, but they should be things that get you "up," not stress you out.

- Do the things that are most important to you early in the day. For example, at work – don't answer your e-mails first thing. Save that for later in the day, when you aren't as fresh. Instead, sort them for later and start your day with the most challenging, exciting piece of work that you have to do

- Make your most important phone calls early. You're more likely to catch people at their desks at the beginning of the day.

- Plan the major portion of your day. Review your to-do list and refresh your memory about scheduled meetings or errands. Divide the rest of the day into project segments. These segments will be time estimates, but they will help you focus on how much you can realistically expect to get done.

— Check e-mail throughout the day, sorting it immediately. Read and respond to urgent items and file the rest away for the times you've already scheduled to handle them.

— Wrap up the day and prepare for tomorrow

— Set aside time (either each day or set days of the week) for relaxation. This is a critical element, because you can't maintain maximum output all the time. You need to allow your mind (and body) to "down-shift" and recover. Your idea of relaxation may involve reading, watching a movie, going for a walk, spending time with friends, but find something that allows you to decompress, and do it.

Becoming Tough

Persistence requires toughness. And if you don't think of yourself as tough, don't worry. Toughness is less an innate thing and much more of learned thing. Which means you can learn it too.

I consider toughness to be something akin to a lifestyle choice. You have to choose it and then pursue it. Relentlessly. If you simply decide from this moment forward that you are going to become tough, you have made the first step. And as simple as that sounds, it is a big step. And from here on out it is simply an ongoing process of making tough choices and doing tough things.

Tough thinking is your ability to use words or mental images to control your emotional state. So tough thinking is actually disciplined thinking. Tough thinking is what keeps you from losing your temper when you make a mistake or from giving up when the battle appears lost.

The thoughts and images you put into your head have precise emotional consequences. And this is why you have to approach your thinking with discipline in mind. Because undisciplined thinking has a tendency to push your goals further and further away from you.

This means you need to take responsibility for what and how you think. When negative thoughts bubble up to the forefront of your mind, you need to understand that they can't take up residence there without your consent. So as soon as you are aware of them, you need to be prepared to serve them with an eviction notice.

One of the simplest yet powerful ways to mitigate negative thoughts is to say "Stop" as soon as these thoughts present themselves. Say "Stop" to yourself and immediately begin inputting positive thoughts and images.

Commit yourself to not allowing negative feelings to lead you into negative thinking. You aren't always responsible for negative feelings, but you are responsible for any negative thinking you permit. Remember, nobody but you is inside your head.

Tough *acting* refers to the use of your body to affect your emotional state. This means disciplined, precise action during whatever challenge you may face. Like tough thinking, tough acting is a powerful weapon with which to manage fear, anger or uncertainty. And this "acting" is completely intertwined with the thinking that must accompany it. If the term acting throws you off or seems odd to you, then let's call it something else. Just call it *pretending*. As in you are pretending to feel confident or strong or capable even when you don't actually feel that way.

I began seriously looking at the connection between the mind and body 20+ years ago when I began teaching a lot of law enforcement and military personnel. And the two big "truths" that I ultimately extracted from all of that time are these:

- "The Form Becomes Its Function."

- "Your Physiology Reinforces Your Psychology."

The first point simply means that you eventually become what you repeatedly do. (This is an idea which goes all the way back to Aristotle.) The adage that "practice makes permanent" is an example of this concept. So, if you build tough ideas into your thinking, those ideas lead to tough decisions, and tough decisions lead to successful outcomes—the kind of outcomes only available to those who are tough. So by taking charge of your thoughts and turning them into tough actions, you can become your own self-fulfilling success prophecy.

The second point is an idea I've championed for almost two decades, which is that "the mind is the body" (which means, conversely, that "the body is the mind"). Research consistently demonstrates the link between a positive/proactive attitude and a healthy (read: **strong**) body. It can be as simple as standing tall, throwing your shoulders back, and casting your eyes confidently towards the horizon. Actually do that and watch your mood change.

"But Mike, what if I don't *feel* confident? What if I am *actually* afraid?"

Great question. *Everyone* is afraid at one time or another. And it's during those times when you feel afraid that you should stand even taller and put on your bravest face. This is how you can use your physiology (your body) to influence your psychology (your thoughts).

Here are some ways to put this idea into action...

- At those times when you feel that your energy is all gone: Force yourself to look as fresh, just like you rolled out of bed on the best day of your life.

- If you've made the worst mistake imaginable: Immediately turn from those negative thoughts and show nothing on the outside but complete confidence.

–   If there is a major crisis approaching: Think calmly. (Don't forget your breathing technique.) Act calm. Become calm.

Don't Play With Fire

In their efforts to act tough or camouflage fear, some people conclude the best way to do this is to **get mad**. And if you have a sports background, this may sound very familiar to you. There are actually a number of coaches who exhort their athletes to "just get mad!" These coaches believe that anger is an effective tool for motivation.

There are some holes in this theory, the largest of which is that anger is a negative emotion. So these coaches (and quite a few other people) end up deliberately anchoring negative emotions to activities that were ostensibly selected for their positive benefits.

To put this another way, let's imagine that eight-year-old Timmy plays the violin. And let's say that Timmy is struggling to master a complicated passage of music. Can you imagine Timmy's violin teacher yelling, "C'mon, Timmy! Get mad! Get *real* mad! That violin can't beat you! I want you to *crush* that violin! Stomp it on the ground!"

And while this may sound completely ridiculous in the context of playing a musical instrument, many people seem to accept this approach in competitive sports. And therein lies the beginning of a long-term problem.

People who fuel their efforts with negative emotion do not achieve a productive mindset. Negativity and anger typically are used to drive nervousness away. And, unfortunately, it works. But once a person does this, the temptation to keep on using negative feelings to control their anxiety level can be hard to resist. And almost without realizing it, negativity gets completely woven into your performance matrix.

Negative emotions flow in two directions: internally and externally. Internalizing negativity via self-directed anger disrupts your immediate performance and long-term results profoundly. Trying to power up your performance with anger is much like throwing gasoline on a fire to keep it going. You will get a big fire, but it will be short-lived and unmanageable. Feeling negative or "out of control" is the antithesis of what we want to accomplish. **Mind Boss** is about fueling your ambitions with *positive* emotion.

Here's another example of teachable toughness. Take a moment to consider the military, where I spent several years learning a great deal about toughness....

The military has a proven system of toughening up individuals. They start with undisciplined and often unmotivated teenagers. Yet over the course of eight weeks, with a clear set of externally imposed standards, the military transforms them into soldiers who are mentally tough—tough enough to confront extreme hardship and fear.

How do they do it? There's actually a lot to it: group psychology, learning new skills, behavioral modelling, recalibrating collective priorities, and of course a lot of yelling. But let's focus our attention on just one thing. Marching. Soldiers in training spend a lot of time marching. How come?

Consider that it has been over a hundred years since soldiers marched in formation onto the battlefield to confront the enemy. Yet despite its lack of applicability in modern combat, soldiers still march. Why? Because marching prepares soldiers for battle.

Marching is more than just walking around. Consider how soldiers marching look on the outside—no visible signs of fatigue or fear. What you do see is discipline and toughness. Marching prepares soldiers for battle by making them practice looking strong and confident even when they don't feel that way. In other words, soldiers learn to "act" tough. Marching produces discipline by teaching concentration and composure, which are essential to overcoming fear (and essential for attaining success in any endeavor).

Happily (at least for most people), you don't have to join the military to use these same techniques that have proved successful for so many years. The structure of daily discipline, planning the day's tasks, regular exercise, and consistent sleep and nutritional practices are all things you can start implementing right away to become more successful.

Accepting Adversity

When people come face to face with adversity is also when many people give up. This may go back to so many people having been raised in a self-esteem culture, but whatever the root of the problem is, it needs to be fixed. And we can fix it by adjusting the way in which we choose to perceive the obstacles in our path.

As we discussed back in Chapter Two, the way you *feel* about a situation may actually be at odds with reality.

Have you ever had to do one of those jobs that looked like it was going to take you a week to complete, but then when you started, you found it was not nearly as difficult as you thought it would be and it actually only took you a couple of days to finish? Our perceptions and assumptions can be deceptive things.

Practitioners of tough thinking see things for what they are. This does not mean they are never affected by emotions or negative circumstances. What it does mean is that they are very good at recognizing those times when external negativity is at work, and when it is, they immediately take action to exert positive control over their thoughts and feelings so they can get back to being at their best.

The Mind Boss approach *is* different, primarily because so many people have grown accustomed to feeling out of control, which is why so many people make statements like, "I can't help the way I feel."

Actually, yes you can. As the boss of your mind, you are in charge. You tell your body (via your brain) what to do. And the truth is that you can choose to feel and think what you want to at any given moment in time. It just takes you deciding to do it and then practicing. And once you start, overcoming adversity becomes a lot easier.

Let's try it right now.

If I asked you to feel really BAD right now, could you do it?

Absolutely. All you would have to do is simply re-live a very negative event you experienced sometime in your life. And if you were to do this with focus and concentration, you will feel bad.

Similarly, if I asked you to feel really GOOD right now, could you do that?

Of course, it works the same way, only in reverse. If you re-live a very positive experience that happened in your life and if you inject those thoughts with enough emotional content, you will feel good.

Being able to positively control your thoughts and feelings in this way is a powerful thing. And like everything else discussed in **Mind Boss**, these are all learnable skills.

One of the key reasons to exert control over your feelings is because feelings influence your decisions...so when something negative happens and you fail to control your emotional state, it becomes very easy to *feel* terrible about the situation and give up.

To overcome the inevitable adversities of life, take a mental step back from the situation and *reframe* it. To reframe means to change the way you currently see things. You do this by finding an alternative perspective or point of view with which to process what is known about the situation. So step back, reframe what you are experiencing, and start to create a new set of feelings.

Here's an example.

Fred is an entrepreneur. Let's imagine that Fred has set up a new business and in his first 6 months he conservatively predicts a $10,000 profit.

However, Fred actually ends up losing $10,000 in his first 6 months.

When faced with a situation like Fred's, many people will *feel* like they have failed—even worse, that they failed very fast. And this is when they are likely to give up on dreams like Fred's new business venture.

Now let's imagine that Fred takes a step back from the situation in order to reframe his thinking. The result is that Fred starts thinking thoughts like these:

- I feel bad right now. I feel bad because I've lost $10,000. But I can see some positives in this situation, too...

- I had over $250,000 in total sales.

- I sold a lot of product. So I know there is a market for what I'm doing.

- I received 94% positive customer feedback. So I also know that my product is of high value and my customers like it.

With this new perspective about how things really are – Fred starts to feel much better about his situation.

The $10,000 loss was significant, but it was just one part of the bigger picture—a picture that also included many positives. Sometimes the difference between success and failure is more a matter of perspective. And persistence.

Persistence is a quality that really makes itself apparent over time. It is about having the capacity to hold up despite disappointments, to endure mind-numbing monotony when your goals seem to get further and further away. And to be able to look at circumstances with fresh eyes and a fresh mind when necessary. And of course it can help to be reminded that others have been where you are—others who persisted and ultimately prevailed.

Here is a tale of persistence personified. It is the story of a young man from Indiana. His name was Harland and he grew up on a farm, the oldest of several children. When Harland was just six years old, his father died from a sudden illness. He then found himself in charge of his younger siblings so that his mother could work to support the family. His school work began to take a back seat to daily tasks like cleaning and cooking meals.

Harlan was 13 when his mother remarried and he immediately clashed with his new stepfather–so much so, that he left home soon afterward. He worked briefly as a farmhand before enlisting in the Army, something which required a significant lie about his age.

After completing his military service (at age 16 no less), he moved to Alabama and found work with a local railroad. He got married at age 18 and started a family.

Harland was fired from his job for insubordination. He found another railroad job in Illinois but was fired after fighting with a coworker. His next railroad job was in Tennessee. While working at this job, Harland began to study law in the evenings through La Salle Extension University.

Harland went on to practice law for three years in Little Rock, Arkansas. But his legal career came to an abrupt end after he engaged in a courtroom brawl with one of his own clients. So Harland found another railroad job. He then left that position for a job selling life insurance only to get fired, once again for insubordination.

Harland then established a ferry boat company which took passengers across the river between Jeffersonville and Louisville, Kentucky. This business was actually successful and he later sold it to finance a new company that manufactured acetylene lamps. This business failed.

Harland then moved to Winchester, Kentucky to work as a sales-man for the Michelin Tire Company. A short time later Michelin closed this facility and Harland was again out of a job. He found another job as the manager of a service station. Several years later this service station went out of business.

In 1930, Harland began working at another service station which allowed him to live rent-free in an adjacent cottage. Harland had been looking for ways to boost his income. He had learned to cook when he was six years old and cooked meals for his siblings. So Harland began preparing meals to sell his customers who had stopped for gas. His specialties were steak, country ham, and chicken. Since he did not have an actual restaurant, he served customers in his tiny living quarters.

Harland's meals became a local hit and in 1939, food critic Duncan Hines visited Harland's modest operation and was impressed enough to include it in his book *Adventures in Good Eating; a Guide to Restaurants Throughout the United States.*

In 1939 Harland acquired a motel in Asheville, North Carolina to which he added a restaurant. Within a year's time both were destroyed in a fire, leaving Harland to rebuild. By this time he had begun experimenting with a new way to fry chicken. He used a pressure fryer, which cooked the chicken much faster than pan frying. The chicken was a hit, but as World War ll broke out, gas rationing had gone into effect. So tourism dried up and Harland was forced to close his hotel operation. He had a string of jobs after that. He was a restaurant manager in Seattle, a government cafeteria manager in Tennessee and then a restaurant manager in Oak Ridge, Tennessee.

Harland continued to perfect his method of chicken preparation and in 1952 he franchised "Kentucky Fried Chicken" for the first time, to a restaurateur in Utah. The chicken was extremely popular, but when a new interstate opened nearby, the reduction in local traffic forced this restaurant to close too. Harland was now 65 years old.

After the Utah restaurant closed, Harland focused on franchising his chicken concept in earnest. He began by traveling from city to city in his station wagon. And in his station wagon Harland prepared chicken in a pressure fryer for prospective investors to sample.

Harland's persistence ultimately paid off. By 1964, Harland, better known as "Colonel Sanders" sold the KFC Corporation, which had become the world's largest chain of chicken restaurants.

There are several lessons in this story. Lessons of persistence, big goals, hard work, proactivity, and more persistence. Interestingly, many years earlier, when Harland was fired from his very first railroad job, his wife had left him. She informed him of that fact in a letter, a letter in which she proclaimed that he would "never amount to anything."

Persistently Proactive

The objective of **Mind Boss** is to provide you with protocols to set your own course and to seize the initiative whenever possible—in other words, to be *proactive*. Being proactive allows you to exert the greatest possible influence over a situation. It is a foundational trait of powerful living. This is because the words with which you frame your thoughts play an active role in situational outcomes. Your spoken words, along with the unspoken words of your mind, position you to be either proactive or reactive in your thinking. The words we use and the (mental) pictures we project truly have power. So they should be chosen carefully.

Let's take a look at what "proactive" means: "*Serving to prepare for, or control an expected occurrence or situation, especially a negative or difficult one....*"

And here is the definition for "reactive": "*Tending to react, pertaining to or characterized by reaction....*"

Now which one of these sounds like the description of someone who can blast through obstacles on the way to reaching their goals?

Here is a scenario that illustrates how the words we choose affect our ability to be proactive or to simply default to reactive thinking. Read it carefully and visualize the situation as it unfolds, trying to really imagine yourself as the person being attacked.

Scenario One:

You are in an isolated area. A large man approaches you in an aggressive manner. You have no doubt that he is intent on attacking you, so you brace yourself for the violence to come. In the dim light you see what looks like a tire iron in his hand. He swings. You throw your right hand up to block....

How did you feel at that moment? Fearful? Uncertain? If this situation were to continue playing out, how do you see it ending?

Now, repeat the same scenario, but this time using different words. Again, really try to see yourself in the situation as it unfolds.

Scenario Two:

You are in an isolated area. A large, aggressive-looking man is coming quickly toward you. There is no doubt that he has criminal intent. You make the decision to strike if necessary and close your fist around the car keys in your hand, leaving the points of several keys protruding from the base of your fist. In the dim light, you see what looks like a tire-iron in his hand. He swings. You strike into his bicep muscle with the tips of the car keys so hard that he drops the tire-iron. You reach down and pick up the tire-iron as he runs away....

Now which of these scenarios would you rather "star" in? The critical difference between the two is that in the first example you were thinking *reactively*. You waited for the assailant to initiate an action and then, at the last minute, you threw up your arm.

But in the second scenario, there was a proactive response to the situation. You were *striking* with your arm rather than blocking. This is a critical distinction. Remarkably, though, the movements were almost the same. In both cases you threw out your right arm. But the thought processes that initiated your arm movement completely affected the outcome (as well as the associated emotional content) of both situations.

The *Proactive* (Tough) Response: You were seizing control of the situation.

The *Reactive* (Un-Tough) Response: You were just preparing to get hit.

To put it another way, in life you can either be the hammer or the nail. And most people don't realize that these roles are not pre-determined. By thinking "tough," you *choose* to be the hammer. Un-tough thinking results in defaulting to the role of the nail. Thinking proactively gives you the opportunity to determine the outcome of a situation. So don't let things just happen to you. Seize the initiative and *make* things happen.

Exercise: The PERSISTENT Mind

One of the simplest ways to enhance **PERSISTENCE** (toughness) is through the mechanism of intense physical training. Physical training works effectively for this because it is a quantifiable and adjustable process. And because it is infinitely variable, it works as an accurate toughness gauge regardless of how well-conditioned a person is.

For people who are primarily physical creatures (competitive athletes), the chief divider between the average and elite athlete is
the degree to which they can withstand the discomfort of rigor-
ous training. The successful athlete is the one who has mastered
the notion of "becoming comfortable with being uncomfortable."
In fact, the secret behind many feats of strength is not strength
itself. There are many people who are very strong. Rather, the
chief variable in doing things like bending horseshoes is pain tol-
erance. Beyond the prerequisite of strength, one has to really
want to bend a horseshoe in order to do it. This is because you
must overcome the extreme pain caused by forcing the steel edge
of that horseshoe into your upper thigh hard enough that you
can create a fulcrum stable enough to force the ends open. It really is about being comfortable with being uncomfortable.

Of course not everyone reading **Mind Boss** is physically ready,
right now, to subject themselves to vigorous physical challenges.
So here is an exercise that provides a physical and mental challenge that is both measurable and completely safe. I was introduced to this exercise by Guy Savelli, the man whose unique abilities served as the inspiration for both the book and subsequent
Hollywood film *The Men Who Stare at Goats*. It simply requires a
candle, a hand-held stopwatch, and a darkened room.

To perform the exercise, seat yourself comfortably in a chair approximately six feet from a lit candle. Hold the stopwatch in your
hand and close your eyes. At the moment you open your eyes,

begin to stare directly at the candle flame and start the stop-watch. The object is to stare at the candle flame as long as you possibly can without blinking.

Savelli instructs his students to keep their jaw clenched and to look directly at the "meat" of the flame. The upper portion of the flame is susceptible to drafts and can move around. This movement is distracting to the eyes and should be avoided.

You will notice that your eyes become uncomfortable during this exercise. They may itch or begin to water. Once your eyes finally blink, hit the stopwatch and then record your time. Practice this once a day and notice that your times will steadily increase. Each time you go a little longer, you are training your mind and body to exceed previous limits. You are teaching yourself toughness, the art of persistence. This is valuable learning.

Three Suggestions

i. Remind yourself, (as often as necessary) of your big goal. When the going gets tough, it is easy to become mired in the moment, feeling as though everything is against you. Don't give up. Step back from the situation and remind yourself why you are doing what you are doing. Remind yourself of your **big goal**.

ii. Difficult things happen. Reframe negative circumstances as temporary challenges. They are all prospectively teachable moments. Never say "I can't" or "I hate." These are examples of un-tough thinking. This is the language of defeat.

iii. Think in the **strongest** possible terms…

"I will be accountable every day."

"I am tougher than any situation that I face."

"I will not defeat myself."

"I will live with integrity."

"I will achieve any goal I set for myself."

CHAPTER 5: PAYOFF

"If you want to live a happy life, tie it to a goal, not to people or things...."
Albert Einstein

Payoff - The Fifth Tenet of Tough Thinking

Payoff. The word itself suggests a tangible reward. And after toiling with ruthless precision and relentless persistence, there is nothing quite so rewarding as finally accomplishing an amazing and audacious goal. If you diligently follow the steps outlined in **Mind Boss** and take massive action, I fully expect you to reach your goals, again and again.

This chapter is different from the others because we won't be discussing "how-to" information. You have already learned what you need to do and how to do it. In this chapter we will instead talk about "why-to" information. Because understanding the "why" of things is the path to true success.

Much of this chapter falls into the "words of wisdom" category, which is a more elegant way of describing regular old advice. Imagine for a moment that you are back in your teens. (If you are presently in your teens, this should be easy to do.) Now think of **Mind Boss** as the family car. And reading **Mind Boss**, has, in essence, taught you how to drive that car. Now imagine I am standing by the door that leads to the driveway. I have the car keys in my hand, but before I hand them to you, I will share some final bits of fatherly advice. Because *my* goal is to set you up for success.

We are going to bring things full circle. At the beginning of **Mind Boss** we learned about goals and goal-setting. Goals are the root of the **Mind Boss** approach; they are the drivers. Now that we are nearing the end, we come back to goals. In its ideal form, this is a circular path. Ideas become goals, goals become plans, plans become accomplishments, and accomplishments create the momentum that leads to larger, more meaningful goals.

Go BIG With Your Goals

So imagine that you are ready to get started—ready to select your first goal using the steps in **Mind Boss**. You found someplace quiet to work and you have seated yourself at a table. Things are just about to get going when you hear a knock at the door. You go to the door and see that it's me. Yes, I have stopped by to help out. And now we are going to have a discussion about your goals.

How will we do this? Very simply, I am going to get things started by asking you some questions. Don't worry, the questions aren't long or complicated. But they are serious. So I'd like you to seriously consider each one before answering. Now, since I can't actually sit down with you to do this, I have listed out the questions below. Take a minute and read through them. It also works well to have someone else read them out loud so that you can consider each one and not get distracted by the next question coming up. This person can also assist you in capturing your answers.

If you have only "you" available, that's fine. This is still a very productive process to work through on your own. Contemplate your thoughts about each question and then record your answers.

Here are the questions...

- What do you want?

- How would you like it to be?

- What is in the way?

- What does this mean to you?

- Is anything holding you back?

- What is stopping you from taking action?

- If you weren't afraid, what would you do?

- Why does this matter?

These are not lightweight questions. They are serious. They are designed to get you thinking about goals in a big way. A life-changing way. And your goals can be just that...amazing, audacious things that change your life. But they can do that only if you have the courage to let them.

Now understand something. You may have had a goal of saving up enough money for a new mountain bike. That's fine. Not every goal needs to be an epic, life-changing quest. Saving up for a mountain bike or new espresso machine is great. But at the same time I want you to be open to the idea that once you start living your life in an intentional, focused way, very big things become possible for you.

Results? What Results?

As we continue this "advanced" discussion of goals, I want you to understand about the pitfalls associated with orienting your goals in the wrong way. This is because it is possible to take a very positive-sounding objective and turn it into a frustration-laden, failure-inducing goal.

I often see this tendency when working with athletes. The world of sports is a mathematical one, where success is easily quantified on a numerical scale. So here is a sports example to illustrate first the problem, and then the solution.

Here is the hypothetical goal: "Next year I am going to win a gold medal in (fill-in-the-blank sport)."

This goal *sounds* good. It's positive, forward-looking, and it's big. So it seems as though it would motivate the athlete in question. And it probably would, for a while. But there is a problem with this goal, which has to do with its focus.

The focus of this goal is on the score and on winning the competition. But an athlete cannot control what score wins the competition. They cannot control what their competitors will do or even what the judges or other officials might do. This means that by trying to pursue this particular goal, they have built their performance criteria around variables that they have no influence over.

There is a term for this type of a goal-orientation; it is called an outcome-based goal. A gold medal is an outcome. A national championship is an outcome. And as outcomes go, these outcomes are ultra-specific. I do not recommend outcome-based goals.

There is a better way of doing things. Instead, the athlete should think about those things that they *can* control, rather than the things that they *can't*. So what would some of those "controllable" things be?

An athlete **can** control:

  — how often they train

  — how long they train

  — the discipline of their efforts

— what they eat

— how they sleep

— what they choose to think about

You get the idea. So how do we take the things that an athlete can control and turn them into an effective goal?

By modifying the previous goal just slightly: "Next year I want to *be capable of* winning a gold medal in (fill-in-the-blank sport)."

It's a very subtle difference in the wording, but it is vastly different in its implications. This new goal is oriented toward the athlete becoming better. By becoming the best athlete that they can be, our athlete might just win a gold medal. But even if they don't, the athlete has left nothing to chance and should have nothing but positive feelings about their new level of capability.

This second type of goal is called a process-based goal. Process-based goals focus on the *process* of becoming better at something. So a process-based goal within a given sport would be geared to producing the most improvements across multiple categories of an athlete's performance.

The other benefit of framing your objectives as process-oriented goals is that this will usually lead to improvements in the process itself. This could be reflected in improvements in the training methods which are used, recovery methods, corrective therapies, injury prevention, nutrition, and so on.

For the greatest "payoff" from *your* goals, build those goals around variables that you *can* control. Structure your goals and subsequent planning around a process. Then begin the work of making yourself as well as your process better.

Signs of Success

I have already mentioned my previous work as a bodyguard. For a five-year stretch I was actively involved in the close-protection field, not only as a bodyguard, but as a trainer of other close-protection teams. And during those five years I was regularly within arm's reach of the "rich and famous"…in their homes, their cars and their private jets. I took care of these VIPs along with their spouses and children.

One of the most distinctive things about the bodyguard profession is the element of physical proximity. Another is the degree to which you become involved with the inner workings of the public and private life of a client.

This work has provided me a vantage point from which I have viewed success up close. And though I am contractually unable to mention most of their names, what I can say is that I have had the rare opportunity to look upon the most significant examples of success that this world has to offer.

Or have I?

The interesting thing about success is that it has more than one

definition. Many more. And yet how many people find themselves pursuing someone else's definition of success rather than
their own?

Much of the time we talk about things as though we know how we
would feel or think if we found ourselves in a particular situation.
And I think that in many cases, these preconceptions are wrong.
People act in all kinds of unexpected ways amidst the stress of an
argument in a grocery store or in the middle of a car crash. And
I have personally seen people act in all kinds of odd ways when
they encounter a celebrity in real life.

So we tend to think that we know how *we* would deal with being wealthy, if we could "finally" have whatever we want. But as
someone who was watched this scenario play out first hand, I will
tell you that having all of that stuff and all of those options is
much more of a challenge than you might think. I have seen the
same vindictiveness, insecurity, and emptiness on display inside
the mansions of billionaires as I did in the low-income neighbor-
hoods and trailer parks that I used to patrol as a police officer.

In short, having cool stuff is cool. But if you're not cool without
cool stuff, then no amount of cool stuff will ever make you cool.

Three Suggestions

i. **Understand That Goals Change Over Time.** As you embark
on the journey of accomplishment, you may find that
over time, a longer-term goal just isn't "speaking" to you

the way it did when you first started out. That's fine. You change over time and your goals are going to change as well. Don't think of adjusted goals as mistakes. Think of them as the inevitable course corrections that occur as you navigate your life.

ii. **Recognize Success.** The first key to recognizing success is knowing what it looks like. One of the problems with chasing other people's ideas of success is that it probably won't look like your definition of success, which might mean that you ultimately arrive at the wrong destination with the wrong accomplishments. This is your journey, no one else's. Determine your target and then fire away.

iii. **Share Your Success.** One of the greatest rewards on the path of accomplishment is how journeying along this path changes you. As you engage in a process designed to make you better, it should come as no surprise that you will become better. You will be a stronger, more decisive person, someone who is confident but grounded. Now who else in your circle of influence would benefit from being around someone who exhibits these qualities? That's right, all of them. So let your accomplishments be an example of excellence and encouragement to others.

In Closing

My goal with **Mind Boss** is to help people learn how to develop a strong, intentional mindset. A mindset that is foundational to the attainment of meaningful goals. Because it is in the pursuit of worthy goals that we find ourselves building lives of meaning.

In this book I have shared more than just techniques and methods, I have shared chunks of my personal story. And the reason for this is to validate what I am teaching you to do. I am a lead-from-the-front kind of person and I wouldn't tell you to do something that I wouldn't do, or to try something that I haven't already tested myself. It's an integrity issue for me.

There's another reason that there is so much "Mike Gillette" in this book. It's because my rather unusual life serves as an example of how "what you've been" should not limit "who you can become." I was a small, scrawny kid–the proverbial 98-pound weakling. I was afraid of everything and everyone. And my frame of reference for family life was a dysfunctional catastrophe.

But that is not me now. Everything which was negative in my life has been reversed. And the best part has not been what I have been able to accomplish. The best part is what I am able to share with others. This book is part of that sharing.

I have one more story to share. It describes some of the struggles I experienced early on. When I was young I had a young person's perspective of how the world worked. I expected that working hard and doing well would yield positive and immediate rewards. I expected to get what I thought I deserved. So many years ago, when I was thrown off course by the injuries I incurred from a rock-climbing accident, my perspective was lacking. But in time I realized that those injuries and the four-plus years it took me to get over them are part of what makes me who I am. And I wouldn't undo them now any more than I would undo the grim circumstances of my early years. This last story is about the changing nature of circumstances and how we respond to those changes, for good or ill.

Many years ago I was lost. And then I was found. And shortly thereafter I was presented with a picture. It just came to me. It was a picture of who I could eventually be. And almost immediately, I wanted to be the person in that picture more than anything else.

The picture was remarkably lacking in specifics. It contained no expository information, no road map. I wasn't entirely sure that there was even a name for what I was looking at. But somehow, I knew that if I could just get to the "place" where the picture appeared to have been taken, then I would know what I was supposed to know and would accomplish what it was I was supposed to accomplish.

Fortunately I was young enough that none of this seemed particularly crazy. The picture was so clear to me in those days that I assumed the picture depicted my "destiny." And I thought as long as I pursued being the man in the picture that things would fall into place. So I expected a smooth path. (Because I was young.)

But this made my life difficult...difficult because things happened, things that pulled that picture from my grasp and hurled it so far away I didn't even know where to start looking for it again.

And during those years I grew to hate that picture. Because the picture was of a man who was physically gifted–someone capable of difficult things, even dangerous things. And in those years my physical self had been taken from me.

Early on into my journey I had become physically broken and I was told that I was unrepairable. So I was confused. I didn't understand why that picture had been such an important part of my life. The man in the picture no longer matched my circumstances or my capabilities. And I didn't understand why it had left just as suddenly as it had arrived. That was the most painful part. Because it never really did leave. It was always so clear in my mind. Always just "there."

In time I found the picture again. And as more time passed I was able start reclaiming my physical self. And this caused the image in the picture to become clearer. I didn't always "know" what I was looking at, but I knew that I was finally on the path that would take me there. But there was one thing that I never really had a clear sense of…the timetable. *When* would I get there?

Years ago, if you had asked me if I would be the man in the picture by age 30, I would have said, "Probably." By 35? "Definitely." How about 40? "Of course. Because the man in the picture couldn't be *that* old.…" But today, in my 50s, I gratefully acknowledge a life that still challenges me, a life that allows me to attain goals that could have been logically dismissed years ago as being far too unreasonable.

Perhaps the best thing about my long pursuit of the man in the picture is, as I said, the picture had always been lacking in specifics. If I'd had any idea way back at the beginning of all the things I would have to do to become that person, I'm quite certain that I would have declined this journey. It would have just seemed far too much to be able to do.

The picture is still in front of me. It's very close. Every day, more and more detail comes into view. But it remains a work in progress. And thankfully, an amazing and audacious one.

I wish you great success in the pursuit of your amazing and audacious goals.

And if you're ready, here are those car keys...

CODA: FUEL FOR THOUGHT...

As I began work on **Mind Boss**, I shared with some friends and colleagues that I was writing a book. Once they learned this, I had a number of requests to include some of what was referred to as my motivational quotes. So here is a collection of my own quotes, specifically selected for you as a reader of **Mind Boss**. I hope they encourage you on your journey.

> *You are in charge of you. So be a good boss.*

> *Toughness is reflected in what you choose to focus on. Some people focus on problems. Tough people focus on possibilities.*

> *Beware of self-fulfilling prophecies. Your brain trusts you. If you keep telling it bad things about you, it will start to believe you.*

> *We tend to get what we expect. Expect better.*

> *Stop focusing on what's "wrong" with you. Start focusing on what's **right** with you.*

There's you and there's the world. And the world isn't fair. You can choose to be unhappy about that fact. But the world isn't unfair either. The world is simply how the world is. You are the variable. You can choose to be unhappy about that fact. Or....

Faults are conspicuous. Both yours and mine. Easy to see, yet hard to see past. If they are all we focus on, we end up disappointed. In ourselves and each other. If everything you see disappoints you, change your focus.

Whatever you are inspired to do, the accomplishment is yours. Whatever you are forced to do, the accomplishment belongs to someone else. Own what you want to achieve so that you may own your results.

We've all heard the phrase "Don't look down." If you're up high and afraid, that's good advice. Don't focus on the thing that causes your fear, it only leads to panic. But if all you do is avoid looking down, you're not making progress. Here's better advice: "Look where you want to go." Managing fear is important, but you still have things to do.

Complacency: An incarcerating state in which you become comfortable being comfortable. If you ever see complacency in the distance, don't wait for it to come closer. Kill it immediately.

Tough people are rare. People navigate toward comfort. Comfort does not build toughness. Be rare.

Feeling courageous is not as important as acting coura-geous. To act courageous, all you have to do is that thing that scares you. It doesn't mean that you're not still scared, it just means that you're going to do that thing anyway. Ex-hibiting courage is a trained skill. The more often it is prac-ticed, the easier it becomes.

Toughness and tenderness are not mutually exclusive quali-ties. It actually takes plenty of the former in order to consis-tently demonstrate the latter.

It isn't enough to simply not "give up." Anyone can dial back effort in order to keep up the appearance of work. But that kind of effort is hollow; it lacks integrity. Effort is meaning-ful when it costs something. It is even more meaningful when it costs everything.

Hold on. A big part of success is simply holding on. It is important to hold on. But it's even more important to under-stand what you're holding on to.

Undoubtedly I have been blessed with many opportunities for achievement. But I also believe that most people are similarly blessed, whether they see those opportunities or not.

The most important skill is to be able to dream far beyond your current abilities.

You might be your biggest problem. You could also be your greatest solution.

For me, rejection has never equaled failure. Not even failure has ever equaled failure.

In real life, there are no "lifeguards on duty." So what will you do? Will you swim? Or will you stand safely on the shore? I prefer to swim.

Forward momentum is easy to maintain compared to the effort required to get started. But only those brave enough to start ever learn this.

Sometimes pain is the necessary currency when purchasing your dreams.

*When I was young I saw myself as weak. And so I remained weak–physically weak, and I made weak (negative) decisions. I had to first envision the idea that I was someone who could become strong before it ever began to happen. If your mind won't accept something as a "real" possibility, then that possibility will never become **real**.*

Anger? I actually like anger if it serves as a catalyst for action. But when it only leads to complaining, followed by inaction – that's when I'm not a fan.

Confidence is overrated. People assume high achievers are perpetually confident. Not true. Stop waiting for the "perfect" moment to have the "perfect" attitude about doing what you want to do. The "perfect" moment is NOW.

Why is it so important to attend to quality-of-life issues? So that you can live a life of quality.

Beware the self-fulfilling prophecy. Your brain trusts you. If you keep telling it bad things about yourself, it will start to believe you.

The way of anger is the way of the lazy. To remain positive, despite the world's problems, requires strength. Anger is effortless. It reflects neither insight nor intellect. The world will always be a tough place. Your outlook is a choice. Choose to be strong.

The REWARDS of discipline are only available to those who submit to the RIGORS of discipline.

Being strong (both inside and out) is entirely dependent on your choices. Choices can be strong or weak. Each choice you make brings you closer or further away from being strong. Therefore, every choice is important.

Be intentional. Things should not, as a matter of routine, take you by surprise. Plan well, follow your plan, and your success will not be an accident of chance.

What goes on inside your head comes out in what you do. Strong thoughts fuel strong deeds.

Expect excellence from yourself so that you may exemplify excellence to others. Encourage excellence in others and be enriched by their example of excellence.

You are, right now, working on your own life story. Do not delegate the task of writing it to others. Each of us is responsible for our own "Happily Ever After."